THE HIDDEN HISTORY

OF THE

EQUAL RIGHTS AMENDMENT

By Hal Draper
and Stephen F. Diamond

To a friend
and
comrade

Steve

PO Box 626
Alameda CA 94501
www.socialisthistory.org
info@socialisthistory.org

ISBN-13: 978-1500182212
ISBN-10: 1500182214

Center
for
Socialist
History

Authors: Hal Draper
         Stephen F. Diamond

Editor: E. Haberkern

Editor's Note

The cover displays is a contemporary photo of participants in the Lawrence Textile Strike of 1912.

Led by prominent organizers of the I.W.W. such as Bill Haywood and Elizabeth Gurley Flynn, these largely female immigrant workers were the driving force behind the movement to improve the living conditions of women workers.

And it was these hard fought for gains that the advocates of a "pure" E.R.A. were willing to sacrifice.

It is this upheaval of working women that has been ignored, not to say suppressed, by the current movement.

Contents

Foreword

By Stephen F. Diamond

The hard fought and lost battle for a constitutional amendment on behalf of equal rights for women is all but forgotten. But the class divide within the feminist movement that contributed to its defeat remains and remains a barrier to their ability to achieve full equality with men. Thus, it makes sense that this manuscript, co-authored by this writer and the late Hal Draper, should finally be published.

In our defense it should be pointed out that we made a diligent effort to bring this hidden history to light some years ago. We ran into an unexpected stonewall from the publishing world. Perhaps the problem was best summed up by the editor in chief of a major academic press that had a long track record of publishing material on the American labor movement. He would have loved to publish the manuscript, he explained to us, but if he did he feared he would never be able to publish a work by an academic feminist again. I am hopeful that the audience for the book today will not have a deleterious impact on our publisher, the Center for Socialist History.

What could have possibly explained such concern about our manuscript? In the end, readers can best decide this themselves. But my own best sense of the problem is that the middle class or "bourgeois" feminism that we differentiate here from "working class" or "social" feminism has a concrete interest in convincing its audience there is only one strand of feminism. In doing so, it helps constrain the possible emergence of working class feminism, which in the end represents a threat to the vested interests of the corporate and political elites that dominate our society. And it should be recalled that these elites remain predominantly male.

A very visible demonstration of the problem can be found in Silicon Valley today. In the high technology sector there is an astonishingly small number of women at all levels, from the startup social media firms to the boardrooms of the large public companies. Apple was recently lampooned when one of its famous product rollouts to the media was made entirely by seven white middle-aged men.

Since our manuscript was first completed in the mid-1980s, male dominance of engineering has actually increased significantly. A smaller number of women now earn computer science degrees than in that era while between 2000 and 2011 alone the number of women in the computer industry dropped 8% while the share of men increased 16%. In 2010, women headed up only 6% of the startup companies financed by venture capital firms.[1]

In the face of this problem, it is astonishing that some of the few women who have reached the senior executive ranks in technology blame women themselves as opposed to deeper structural problems in the modern capitalist economy for the problem. Google executive Sheryl Sandberg argues in her new book *Lean In* that women have to be more aggressive in efforts to reach leadership roles in business and government.[2]

Sandberg could have had her fellow Google executive Marissa Mayer in mind as a model when writing the book. Mayer left Google after working her way to the top and earning hundreds of millions of dollars. But it would appear that experience taught her little about the problems facing women in the work place.

In quick order she joined the board of Walmart and became CEO of the troubled search engine Yahoo.

Walmart is notorious for its poor treatment of women workers and has been sued in several states for sex discrimination, sexual harassment and other labor law violations.[3] When confronted about the problem at a recent technology event, Mayer "poked fun" at a small group of female protestors and then laughed while her host, fellow technology CEO Marc Benioff of Salesforce, lauded his "great legal team,"[4] before watching the women escorted out of the event by security.

Mayer herself was pregnant when she began her new role at Yahoo, but initial optimism about what that might mean for employees trying to balance the demands of work and family quickly dissipated as Mayer promptly ended employees' ability to telecommute. Ironically, this was precisely the kind of "flexible work practice" that Sandberg had praised in *Lean In* because it would allow women to advance at companies like Yahoo and therefore "would serve families, and society, well."[5]

Mayer had no such balancing problem of her own, of course, as she simply used a tiny slice of her vast wealth to build a nursery for her newborn child right next to her new executive office.[6]

Sandberg, at least, acknowledges that, "the vast majority of women are struggling to make ends meet and take care of their families."[7] She frankly admits the core of her advice to "lean in" at work will only "be most relevant to women fortunate enough to have choices about how much and when and where to work."[8]

It is to the billions of women around the globe who do not enjoy such choices that this book is dedicated.

Preface:
A Personal View

By Hal Draper

This preface reflects my personal experience, and so it must be written in the singular, though all matters of view and interpretation are shared by the two authors.

The intellectual begetter of this book was Anne Draper; and thereon hangs an essential point.

Anne Draper was, for many years before her death in 1973, one of the ablest of trade-union organizers in this country, working for the Amalgamated Clothing Workers in her last years and before that for the Hatters & Millinery Workers Union. Her work was by no means confined to women workers, but the composition of the two unions' membership gave her an experience in this field which few could match. This was a valuable background, but it was not the experience which impelled her into the subject matter of this book. In between her stints for the above-mentioned two unions, she went to work as research director for the California State Federation of Labor, for about six months. Here she immediately ran into a problem which gave her a brand-new education on the subject of workingwomen.

As the State Fed's research director, she was immediately called on to testify at the hearings routinely organized by the state commissions entrusted with the enforcement of labor laws for women, especially in agricultural labor. She naturally learned all there was to know about these situations, and just as naturally became labor's chief advocate at these hearings. Above all, the problems of workingwomen in the fields hit her very hard, the more she learned of the unbelievable callousness of the agrotycoons to the conditions of their "hands," and also the indifference of many trade unions.

Even after she left the State Fed and went to work as West Coast representative of the Amalgamated Clothing Workers, she continued work on the issue, and to this end helped to establish the first support group for the farm workers' organization efforts (Citizens for Farm Labor, centered in Berkeley). This was well before farm labor became a popular issue among liberals, and before César Chavez's name became well known. (I still have the black-eagle banner which the Farm Workers' Union voted to honor her work.) My own connection with her activity was mainly that of a listening ear as she talked over her problems; what this means is that I received an education too, on the side.[1]

When the contemporary feminist movement started growing, Anne Draper reacted by pioneering the establishment of a new kind of organization for trade-union women. Called Union W.A.G.E., its full name was Union Women's Alliance to Gain Equality. We will come back to its work in the Appendix.

The only labor laws that could be utilized by the farm workers' union and its well-wishers were the existing legislative provisions for *special protection for women workers*. As we will see later, such legislation has often been important, in the history of advancing labor legislation, as an opening wedge: in one way or another, the gains made by women workers were eventually extended to all workers. This pattern has been immensely important to the labor movement. But in particular where working conditions are specially horrendous, the legislation for workingwomen is specially important for reasons far more immediate.

Anne Draper learned very quickly what few city dwellers know, that for workingwomen in the fields, and not only in California, not war but work is hell — a special torment. But nobody wanted to be told that. At first, when she was as ignorant of the facts as most people were, she listened almost in disbelief to the testimony of the women workers at the state commission hearings, testimony mostly given in the foreign accents of Mexican- and Filipino-Americans. Then she came to know their conditions firsthand. All this has to be mentioned for background, but it is still not the present subject.

What is important for us at this point is the following: as the new feminist movement coalesced around the demand for the Equal Rights Amendment, Anne Draper discovered that these alleged feminists were the most vicious and implacable enemies of every goal of decent conditions for which the farm workingwomen were fighting and for which trade-union women had ever fought.

Everyone knows now why this is so: the "New Feminists," largely businesswomen and professional women and other upwardly mobile types, who had taken the E.R.A. as their banner, decided that *every* kind of "special protective legislation" for women had to be rooted out and destroyed on the ground that it was incompatible with their Amendment.

For Anne Draper (and so incidentally for me) the issue was posed most starkly in terms which you, dear reader, may think beneath your dignity and even— well, unrespectable. It was about...Toilets.

For years the workers who pick our cheap vegetables (for cheap wages) had been demanding that the growers provide a minimum amenity for workingwomen who had to spend the whole day working in the fields in order to live, even if they sometimes had to carry their small children along with them. One of the simplest things they asked for was the provision of portable toilets in the fields. And for years this request had been refused by the growers; it would cost too much money. The union did not fail to point out what this meant in terms of sanitation, not only with respect to the workers but also to the farm products; it pointed out, to uninterested employers, that it meant unsanitary products for consumers and a life of humiliation for the farm workers. For all these years the farm workers had been unable to convince the state commissions that *toilets in the fields* were a minimum requirement for decent working conditions.

And now here was a self-styled women's movement that fought just as bitterly as any of the growers' organizations against any legislation in the interest of workingwomen, and threatened to destroy what legislation already existed. A "women's movement"? Movement of *which* women?

Anne Draper was well acquainted with university women who were fighting against sex discrimination in the appointment and promotion of professors. In fact she had been involved in the first attempts to establish a local of the Teachers Union on the Berkeley campus of the University of California, one of whose main aims would be to oppose sex discrimination. Now the E.R.A. feminists were maintaining loudly that equality for women in the professions could not be achieved except on a basis that destroyed the only immediate hope of workingwomen for an improvement of their conditions...

Were toilets in the field really incompatible with sex equality on the university faculty? Did a woman professor have to help destroy the farm workers' efforts in order to be able to make her own demands for justice on the job?

Toilets in the field are a paradigmatic issue in another way. Under the conditions set by circumstances and the authorities, it could be fought for only as a "special protective" law for women workers. *But everyone knew that it could be achieved in practice only as a gain for all workers.* Once the growers had to provide toilets in the fields, no one expected their use to be confined to women. *The union could not win this demand for women without winning it also for all.* And this is what has happened again and again in the history of labor struggles.

For the E.R.A. feminists it was not necessarily only a matter of consistent legalism. Not infrequently (see, for example, the early issues of *Ms* magazine) an erudite woman professor would explain that, morally speaking, it was *insulting* to all womanhood to believe, as the labor movement allegedly did, that women were such paltry weak creatures as to *need* "special protective" devices. They explained that it was the usual assumption of male master-ship. Anne Draper was quite capable of dealing with this profound thought on its own philosophic basis, but she often preferred to ask a different question. Suppose the women professors who wrote this stuff had no women's rooms of their own but had to squat in the school yard... (I warned you that this subject was not respectable.) Well, in short, would the aforesaid women academics feel so confidently philosophic about it all? In fact, this is a sort of "thought experiment," which provides its own solution.

This is being written not long after I read the moving book by Professor Sylvia Hewlett, *A Lesser Life*[2] — a book which is a prerequisite for everyone concerned with this issue. In fact, the title of this preface is deliberately copied from Hewlett's introductory section. It was "A Personal View" for Hewlett not because its viewpoint was peculiar to her, but because it explained how she had actually come to see the issues. In her case, the governing discovery was that a woman was debarred in practice from achieving a career (in her case as a professor of economics) or at least achieving the upper rungs of a career in accordance with her ability, *unless* she gave up any idea of also functioning as a normal mother and wife along the way. In her case, the revelation was the attitude of the E.R.A. feminists toward such a simple demand as *maternity leaves* — a demand, moreover, which she found to be already achieved in most of the advanced countries of the world. (There is much more in Hewlett's book, but maternity leave will suffice as the example of the kind of "special protective" provision which aroused the bitter enmity of the people she knew as "feminists.")

Hewlett does a masterly job of laying out the issues and explaining, both in socioeconomic terms and in human-personal terms, what is wrong with the approach taken by the contemporary American feminist movement. She makes an unanswerable case for the *necessity,* not merely the desirability, of "special protective" provisions for women at work. I would gladly devote a chapter to summarizing her case, except for the belief that you would do much better, dear reader, to read it yourself in all its details. Remember that Hewlett is concerned with, and addresses herself to the lot of, women in professional and business careers much like the women who have put the E.R.A. on their banner; Hewlett's references to the mass of women workers in this country are sympathetic but very few. She has come to her conclusions from a direction entirely different from that of Anne Draper. But more important is this: she comes to a central conclusion in which, alas! she abandons the field of "equal rights" altogether.

This is a deeply disappointing conclusion, even though it takes up little space in her book. It is no doubt utilized by her opponents to help vitiate the rest of her work. They convinced her that she had to choose between "social feminism" and equal rights, and that if she opted for social feminism (as she understood it) she had to let equal rights go.

Anne Draper faced this problem too, of course, but adopted an entirely different solution: a proposed Equal Rights Amendment that did *not* destroy legislation necessary to women workers. She did not have to invent this proposal from scratch; it had come up more than once in the history of the E.R.A., and we will see in the ensuing pages that it has appeared in at least four forms. But Professor Hewlett apparently knows little about the hidden history of the E.R.A. and never refers to the alternative versions of the Amendment. On the other hand, the proposals for a workingwomen's E.R.A. will be important for the present book.

Professor Hewlett's difficulty becomes apparent as she discusses one of the most enlightening cases that showed the meaning of the E.R.A. movement. This was the 1982 case of Lillian Garland, a Los Angeles bank employee who, after bearing a child by Caesarean section, was certified by her doctor as able to return to her job. Only — the bank informed her that her job had been filled and there was no other position open for her. She had not even known that she would have to choose between having a baby and making a living. Evicted from her apartment for lack of money, she lost custody of the child to its father, for lack of resources to care for it.

A state office then decided that the bank had acted illegally, for a 1979 California law gave a woman in her position up to four months of unpaid leave with job maintenance. The bank thereupon challenged the constitutionality of the law, arguing, on "E.R.A. grounds," that it was sex-discriminatory. In this action the bank was joined by the state Chamber of Commerce and the Merchants and Manufacturers Association. And N.O.W.

also jumped in to support this coalition against Garland, with a brief of its own. "Most women's rights groups," says Hewlett, sided with the bank and its employer brigade plus the feminist phalanx. There were over 200 other such cases pending in the state. And she concludes:

> It is my guess that if she [Garland] knew where NOW stands on this issue, she would pass up feminism and throw equal rights out of the window — along with the ERA.[3]

She concludes her chapter with a "lesson": "that feminism should not be equated with equal rights and that sometimes women have to be treated unequally if they are to have a fair deal as mothers and workers."[4] Throughout, she identifies "equal rights" wholly with the E.R.A. as she knows it.

Anne Draper never fell into this trap. She used to argue, in debates with N.O.W.-type feminists, that the word *equal* need not be turned into a code-word meaning *same and identical*. We all know that this is true in many other cases. The male–female difference is distinctive, of course, and so analogies involve problems. But consider: if we are to provide "equal" access to (say) public buildings for all persons regardless of physical differences, does this laudable equality debar us from requiring a ramp approach which would be useful mainly for disabled persons? On the contrary, if disabled persons are *not* provided with a ramp access, do they still enjoy "equality" of access? If this line of thought applies to disablement (which is not usually a natural condition), does it not apply ten times *more* strongly to the natural conditions faced by women in the course of normal lives as mothers and wives? N.O.W.-type debaters, to be sure, angrily denounced this argument as equating femininity with disablement, therefore proving that they were seeing the matter upside-down. The real moral is that femininity, which should have far *more* rights than any deviant physical condition, has been deprived of these rights in our American society, and therefore has been operationally deprived of equality of condition.For women to enjoy *equal* rights with men, they must have *equal opportunity to be different*. It is a male-sexist mind-set to believe that maternity (for example) is an impermissible deviation from normal human conduct, to be shunted off to a specially "disabled" section of the population. Professor Hewlett shows again and again how the E.R.A.-type feminists share with sexist males the same view of a "normal" human life, and why therefore the typical career-woman feels that motherhood and a once-normal family life can be no part of it. Hewlett calls these women "male-clones," and her analysis of this phenomenon is a triumph of thought leavened by experience.

The lines of battle drawn up about the E.R.A. do not show only two camps, only two viewpoints. The choice is not only between the N.O.W.-type feminists and what Professor Hewlett calls a kind of "social feminism" opposed to equal rights. For years there was a third viewpoint prominent among social-feminists, until it was overshadowed by the new sort of feminism that burgeoned in the 1960s. It was this third approach that Anne Draper sought to implement in founding Union W.A.G.E. and allied activities. *Now that E.R.A.-type feminism, along with the E.R.A. itself, is in considerable confusion, it is especially important to listen to this third approach.*

That is what the hidden history of the E.R.A. will serve to show, in the chapters to follow.

1. The Two Kinds of Feminism

The Equal Rights Amendment was launched in 1921 by an offshoot group of the women's suffrage movement, which had achieved its immediate objective two years before with the passage of the nineteenth Amendment. The main front on which the suffragists had fought had now been won: where next? The movement split along lines that had been implicit in the history of the struggle, but not into equal parts. One group of activists, led by Alice Paul, wanted to work out another one-plank platform — a single-shot concentration like the vote issue just won. These people organized themselves as the "National Woman's Party" and decided that their new single shot was going to be a brief and abstract statement of "equal rights" for both sexes, put forward as a constitutional amendment. They were going to be concerned with nothing else.

Most of the then existing women's movement turned in a quite different direction. In this postwar period of new social ferment — of sociopolitical disappointments and hopes — they looked forward to extending their range from narrow interests to important social change and reforms. This tendency is called the *social-feminists** by the historian J. S. Lemons, who has covered this history most profoundly.[1]

One of the pillars of this social-feminism was the Women's Trade Union League, which comprised active trade-unionists and their liberal and leftist allies. Women trade-unionists have always had to fight for women's rights and workingwomen's interests not only against the employers but also against the officialdoms of many unions and against the entrenched

---

* It must be noted that Professor Hewlett, as discussed in the Preface, uses the term *social-feminism* with a meaning and connotation quite different from Lemons: Hewlett *counterposes* any concern with social issues (like maternity leave) to the issue of equal rights. Hewlett's conception of social-feminism is, therefore, as blinkered and stunted a notion as her opponents' conception of abstract equal rights. Lemons makes it historically clear that the social-feminists of the 1920s were proponents of equal rights, but gave equality a more profoundly social interpretation. Our own use of the term will follow Lemons.

prejudices of male workers. (This was still one of the chief reasons for the organization of Union W.A.G.E. even in the 1960s and later.) Another pillar was early formed by the Women's Bureau set up in the Department of Labor as the result of outside pressure. This was a very exceptional case: under an outstanding trade-unionist, Mary Anderson, the Bureau functioned more as an arm of the women's movement than of the current administration, which sought to negate its work by starving it for funds. It should no more be confused with other government departments than the Women's Trade Union League should be confused with Samuel Gompers and the American Federation of Labor — many of whose unions barred women, or discriminated against workingwomen, and usually made only half-hearted efforts to organize them.

In general terms: the social-feminists saw the lot of workingwomen in the forefront of the "woman question" of the day, even in those cases where the feminists themselves were middle-class in origin. One of the leavening influences was the significant socialist women's movement; and indeed this movement liked to think of itself as a workingwomen's movement. In contrast, the other current, crystallizing around the one-plank Amendment, tended to appeal more and more to business and professional women ("career women" so called). And as this current grew in numbers and self-confidence in American life, so also did its type of feminism. It was a self-consciously middle-class feminism, more and more impatient of being held back by the alien needs of the majority working women.

This difference in outlook was concretized above all on the issue of "special protective legislation" for women workers.It was a matter of ABC that trade-union workers fought for immediate economic gains, with whatever weapons they possessed; and it was ABC for women workers as much as for any others. Every more or less militant organization of male workers tried to improve conditions in its special sphere, as well as (theoretically at least) for the working population as a whole. But when this ABC conception was acted out by *women* workers, there was an outcry from certain circles.

In the case of male workers, the question of "special" protective legislation has been so long worked out that it no longer seems to be controversial. "Protection" on the job was and is a typical labor demand. The term has nothing derogatory about it, in origin. Yet protective legislation *for men* was once a difficult issue inside the trade-union movement. It is almost forgotten that, at one time, the leaders of the A.F. of L. attacked the legislative imposition of (say) a minimum wage — on the ground that it would redound against labor's interests. They argued *inter alia* that a minimum wage might tend to become the maximum wage, thereby hurting better-paid workers even if it improved the position of the lowest strata.

There was a kernel of truth to this fear; it could be sensibly maintained by a united front of employers and conservative unionists. For such special protective legislation as a minimum-wage law *could* be used by employers for their own purposes. This argument is of such wide application that it negates itself; for in fact there is no conceivable labor legislation which *cannot* be turned against workers, and which has not indeed been so utilized in the course of its history. We can put this even more strongly: it is well-nigh inevitable that even prolabor legislation will be used in practice against labor's interests *unless* the labor movement is organized to effectively police the way the law is applied. The historical moral is this: labor legislation ("protective legislation") is not a substitute for trade-unionism and workers' organization; it is one weapon of trade unions, and where trade unions do not exist as yet it is an added reason for building them.

In modern experience there has been no lack of cases in which basic labor gains, painfully acquired by decades of struggle, have been used at times by employers (or their allies in the government and trade-union bureaucracies) to discriminate against minority workers and disadvantaged sectors of labor for the benefit of an entrenched job trust. Seniority on the job, as a defense against willful firing, is one of these painfully acquired gains, but everyone knows that the seniority issue has been used to squeeze black workers and other minorities out of the labor market. This issue has had to be met, but from the workers' point of view one way of *not* meeting the issue is to destroy every seniority system holus-bolus and indiscriminately.

No one today argues on principle against "special protective legislation" for *men* workers. There are real problems of application; there are different solutions for various cases; yet no one but the traditional antilabor element advocates that all our labor laws ("protective legislation") be thrown out in a heap and destroyed, turning the clock back more than a hundred years. (For example, through so-called "Right to Work" laws.)

But the picture is altogether different when it comes to special protective legislation for women workers. What is taken for granted on behalf of laboring men is bitterly fought when it comes to laboring women. Why?

The bitter opposition comes not only from employers (who are understandably reluctant to favor any new labor laws for anyone) but also from the middle-class feminists whose core rests on the business and professional career-women primarily.

In this connection there is an analogue with the world of male labor: consider the opposition of traditional "labor aristocracy" elements against upgrading the conditions of unskilled or lesser-skilled labor. The highly skilled and "near-professional" machinist may even feel "degraded" by being regarded as "labor"; it is an elitist mind-set that has played a large part on the negative side of labor history. It is a mind-set that will be immediately recognized by anyone reading about the indignant opposition of professional women to "special protective legislation" designed to benefit their poorer "sisters."

Protective laws for the benefit of women workers in factories or fields may help to make *their* work a little more bearable, but such laws are usually irrelevant to upper-echelon women trying to compete with men in a profession. Worse, these laws may introduce restrictions that get in their way. Sometimes the complaints of the career-women may well be justified, in cases where a poorly drawn law introduces thorough irrelevancies into occupations not targeted by the law. The remedy is plain enough: alleviation of these cases by ad-hoc changes. *But this has not been the course taken by the middle-class feminist movement in America.* Off with their heads! Destroy all these inconveniences to the proper advancement of women-in-competition-with-men! Down with all special laws to help workingwomen! But this sweeping destruction, which is the very point of the E.R.A. as presently formulated, is justified only by a narrow-spirited group egoism. Protective legislation for women workers is denounced, rather abstractly, as a form of "sex discrimination" (or "gender discrimination" in the newer jargon). True, isn't it? To understand this, we should go back to the older days when any labor legislation (primarily for male workers, of course) was routinely labeled a form of "class legislation" and denounced as such. True, wasn't it?

Prolabor legislation is indeed "class legislation" — only, in civilized countries today this is no longer said as a denunciation (in fact, no one bothers to say it). Everybody knows that labor legislation is nothing but an attempt to achieve a slightly closer approach to *equality* on the part of workers. It is not an offense against "equality"; it is a step toward it — and usually a miserably tiny step at that. A law calling for a minimum wage so small that no family can live on it: this is hardly going to revolutionize society, but still it is *class discrimination*. It really is.

If (to hark back to the indecencies of the Preface) women workers in the fields are accorded the amenity of a portable toilet, this will be *sex discrimination* indeed — but these workingwomen will still be light-years from equality. They can yell *Sex discrimination* all they wish, but this sex discrimination is a very tiny step toward equality, not away from it.

Social-feminists have been in the forefront of such causes as opening up medical colleges to female students; if they tend to regard the issues directly affecting the lives of women workers as more important, this is only because the latter affects far more women. There is another side to this picture. The fine women who, rightly and bravely, aspired to crash into the medical profession were to be applauded — and they *have* gotten at least their fair share of applause — but at the same time one must recognize that many of these types tended to look on the "lower" interests of workingwomen as an *embarrassment* to their own lofty cause. There have been too many cases where objectively, like many strivers from the upper strata, they were quite willing to get ahead over the backs of the mass of their sisters. The *best* of them explained that as soon as they had it made, they would do good for the less fortunate; but — first things first; and *they* were the first things...

So even insofar as "special protective legislation" for women workers did in fact provide immediate benefits only to women, it was still a step toward sex equality. And we have already touched on the second link between such legislation and real equality: the tendency for this special legislation to be extended to *all* workers, not only women. This tendency has worked itself out, historically, in several ways.

(1) In the case aforementioned (toilets in the field), the concession itself cannot, by its very nature, be provided only for women; once in existence, it benefits all workers. Another example is the demand for the installation of elevators to obviate a long climb on factory stairs.

(2) There are cases where, once a concession has to be provided to women workers, *economic* considerations make it wise for the employer to provide it also for all.

(3) When the women workers win a concession, this fact alone lends impetus to the men workers (through a trade union or otherwise) to launch a struggle for the same gain, perhaps by union contract rather than legislation. Thus the whole labor front advances by a stride.

(4) On the juridical front, "special" legislation for women workers has often been the entering wedge for a court's approval of advanced social legislation for all.

The social-feminists of the 1920s were exceedingly conscious of these possibilities and their meaning *both* for improvement in workingwomen's conditions and for the furtherance of sex equality in general. Around the turn of the century, Supreme Court decisions had already shown what could happen. In *Holden v. Hardy* — 169 U.S. 366 (1898) — the Court upheld the eight-hour day for coal miners, all men; and to do so, relied for support on state legislative limits of women's working hours. In turn, the *Holden* decision was cited in the Court's opinion in *Muller v. Oregon* — 208 U.S. 412 (1908) — when the ten-hour day for women was upheld. Finally, Felix Frankfurter referred to both of these decisions in his arguments to the Court in *Bunting v. Oregon* — 243 U.S. 426 (1917). The Court agreed with Frankfurter and legalized the ten-hour day for all workers.

At least three out of the four factors listed above were involved, mutually supporting each other, in one of the most famous of American labor struggles: the Lawrence Textile Strike of 1912.

It is remarkable how many labor histories and other works relate the stirring events of this strike movement, including the great role played by I.W.W. organizers, without however mentioning what had precipitated the strike. *This great strike started because of a victory gained in "special protective legislation" for women workers* — a victory which inexorably produced a battle to defend the conditions of all workers, who were engaged in the decades-long drive for a shorter work-day. Here is what happened.

In 1911 the Massachusetts state legislature yielded to labor's pressure on what seemed a minor point: it reduced the maximum work-week for women and under-18 children from 56 to 54 hours. In the textile mills, these workers constituted over fifty percent of the labor force. The Lawrence mill owners announced that, in their calculations, "it would not be economy to manage their force on dissimilar periods of labor," and that the hours reduction would be applied to all workers, men, women and children.Only — there was a catch: the week's pay would be accordingly reduced. Here they were breaking with their own precedent. Two years before this, when they had had to reduce the work-week from 58 to 56 hours, they had changed the hourly wage to maintain the week's take-home pay at the same level. This level was already on the poverty floor, and typically a whole family, husband, wife and child, had to work in the mills in order to maintain an existence. The mill owners were confident that this time the workers were in no position to protest effectively. They found out otherwise, but the story of the great battle is not our subject.[2]

If you look back to the four ways in which special women's gains have led to generalization for all workers, you will see that the Lawrence strike involved the last three, in one form or another. This is quite typical; the cases are seldom "pure." The issue before us is not an exercise in abstract political theory or, even less, abstract ethics. What is typically involved is *interests,* often spelled out in dollars and cents. Even the provision of human dignity, as in the case of toilets in the field, has a price tag for at least one side of the argument. Equality is a great human goal, but it is not merely an abstraction: it too has a price tag in our society.

It will be a good idea to keep this in mind when we see an abstract kind of Equality raised as a banner in 1921.

2 The Original Alliance for the E.R.A.

At about the same time that the group calling itself the National Woman's Party proposed an Equal Rights Amendment as its new one-punch platform, an ominous economic development emerged on the scene in the wake of the First World War's end.

Women had been drawn into the job market by the war; but when it was over, most companies wanted to get rid of them. Men workers, including unionized men, often wanted them out too, since they were economic competition in these uncertain times.

One such company was the Brooklyn Rapid Transit Company, which had employed a large number of women ticket sellers and now wanted to fire them and give their jobs to men. It looked around for a legal pretext, and found one at hand: the new 1919 law against night work for women. It is easy to show that other cities and other companies had found such laws no obstacle to the employment of women *if* the company really wanted to employ them. But when the B.R.T. in this city used the ploy of pointing to labor legislation for women, and made this its pretext for a mass layoff, that was enough for some purposes.

The old arguments against the employment of women were dusted off; and as the dust rose, the onus for the dismissals was laid not on the hardheaded company with its eyes on profits, but was channeled against the advocates of social justice and labor legislation. Some women dismissed from the B.R.T., flanked by some business and professional women, formed a group demagogically called the Equal Opportunity League, to fight the menace of labor legislation for women. This was the best kind of front for an old employers' cause; for its advocates were self-motivated and sincere, and did not have to be paid.[1]

Even today the myth is encountered — especially in the pages of contemporary historians enthusiastic about the E.R.A.

— that the night-work law was to blame for the dismissal of these women workers. The claim is made that the B.R.T. had intended to retain all women workers *and* rehire the returning soldiers, until male-controlled unions pushed through the 1919 law and thus "forced" the company to fire the women.[2] The facts tell a different story. B.R.T. correspondence itself admitted that a hiring freeze on women conductors went into effect as soon as the Armistice was signed, six months before the law went on the books. And throughout that six-month period hundreds of women were laid off.[3]

Testimony by the great women's champion, Mary Anderson, head of the then new Women's Bureau of the Labor Department, brought the foregoing out into the open in 1925, when she testified before the House Judiciary Committee. Speaking against the consequences of the proposed E.R.A., she noted that the B.R.T. tale was still being deployed by antilabor propagandists:

> One question [raised] yesterday was in connection with the Rapid Transit Co. of New York City. In the Rapid Transit Co. during the war many women were employed, and just as soon as the Armistice was signed the company began to discharge the women, and every month they discharged a greater and greater number. The law that affected the women on the R.T. Co. was not introduced until March; so that it was not the law but the after-the-war conditions that were responsible for the general-reduction of the women in the Rapid Transit Co.[4]

The B.R.T. case is the paradigm for the times. We will come back to it again in Chapter 5, to see how the facts were fully investigated for the first time.

Business found it understandably useful to blame the dismissal of wartime women workers on the evil labor legislation which "forced" them to take this step despite their kindly desire to do otherwise, with a noble disregard for profit... Before we give too much credence to this fairy tale, we should understand the pattern behind it.

The target was not merely labor legislation for women. The target was labor legislation (period). For a whole period of time, court decisions had been striking down labor legislation for the *protection* of (men) workers on the ground that such laws violated the rights of property and "liberty of contract." (*Liberty,* of course, was the great desideratum.) This basis for the erasure of whatever labor legislation got through the legislatures had only one loophole in it — but it did have one. From the early years of the century onward, the Supreme Court allowed only laws favoring women workers, on the ground of women's "physical structure," "maternal functions," etc. Through the decade of the 1910s, such labor laws limiting "liberty of contract" made rapid progress, *through being sex-based.*

Now business was in process of discovering a new argument, and a new force, to mobilize against this big hole in its defenses against labor legislation. The historian Lemons summarizes this development:

> The increasingly effective opposition included indus-trial and manufacturers' associations, vengeful anti-feminists, reactionary organizations like the Sentinels of the Republic, some business

and professional women, and extreme feminists of the National Woman's Party. The courts also laid a withering hand on women's protective legislation. The minimum-wage movement advanced until 1923, when, in the name of "liberty of contract," it was nearly struck dead — and the National Woman's Party hailed the defeat as a victory for equal rights.[5]

Readers of Prof. Sylvia Hewlett's *A Lesser Life* will be forcibly reminded of her horrifying discovery — over a half century later — that N.O.W. was supporting and advocating the court decisions destroying legislative provision of maternity leave and job maintenance. In 1923, when the Supreme Court decision declared the minimum wage unconstitutional and the N.W.P. celebrated this great triumph for its cause, the social-feminists were aghast at this revelation that, to the minds of the Pure Equality advocates, it did not matter that tens of thousands of workingwomen were condemned to starvation wages, as long as Mrs. O. H. P. Belmont was spared the "insult" of being "protected" by legislation just like a wretched little seamstress or field picker.

The Paulites did not draw back from the implications of their united front with big business, nor did the National Association of Manufacturers (then perhaps the leading representative of commercial and industrial capital in the country) fail to see how this group of militant women fell in with its aim of stemming the postwar tide of social legislation. The historian Lemons relates:

> The NWP frequently appeared as the chief supporter of the manufacturers' associations' position on labor legislation and thwarted the effort of the other groups to win new protections for working women. The N.A.M. recognized the value of the N.W.P. in defeating labor legislation and endorsed the equal rights amendment in 1923.[6]

Thus one of the most openly reactionary organizations in the country became one of the first to offer official support to the Pure amendment. The political side of this alliance was consummated at the end of 1923: the Pure amendment, now blessed by the guaranteed-antirevolutionary manufacturers' association, was introduced into the Senate by the Republican Party whip, Charles Curtis, a dim machine politician who later became Herbert Hoover's vice-president.

This alliance, plus much else, was acted out at the Second Conference of Women in Industry organized in January 1926 by the Women's Bureau and its Mary Anderson, to take up a number of problems important to the participating women's organizations.

The main headlines on the first day of the conference were devoted to — the president of the National Association of Manufacturers; he denounced legislative interference in industry, "with only the N.W.P. members applauding." The N.A.M. president charged that the women working for a child-labor law were Communist dupes, and that the government's Children's Bureau was promoting the work of a certain Soviet leader named "Madame Kollontai"...

The small N.W.P. contingent, a brigade of about a dozen, was organized to work after a fashion that was made widely known only much later by Communist Party meeting-wrecking-squads. The famous militancy of the Paulites was now pointed, like a gun, against the rest of the women's movement. Through the second day of the conference, the dozen N.W.P.'ers were on their feet with tumultuous demands that the conference be given over to *their* patented demand, the Pure E.R.A. Lemons summarizes the then-unprecedented scene quite calmly:

> All of the dozen NWP members leaped to their feet demanding recognition, supposedly to make short seconding speeches. However, Mabel Vernon [NWP executive secretary] went around exhorting them to "get up and yell — you've got good lungs!" ... Near the end Anita Pollitzer of the NWP rushed over to the press table and asked, "Have we done enough to get into the papers? If we have, we'll stop." Finally a vote was taken on [Gail] Loughlin's [NWP] motion, and it lost by a huge, angry majority.[7]

Even sympathizers of the N.W.P. were alienated if they were in attendance at this operation, but the operation was aimed not at the conquest of innocent bystanders but of the headlines in the press. As far as Alice Paul was concerned, disrupting a conference of serious women's organizations was the same as disrupting a cabinet meeting in order to get headlines for militant suffragists...This National Woman's Party was a split-off from what had been the mass organization of the suffragist movement, the National American Women's Suffrage Association

(N.A.W.S.A.). It first incubated inside NAWSA as a faction; then it split off in 1914, calling itself the Congressional Union; and it finally organized itself under the "party" name in 1916.

The N.W.P. had two distinctive characteristics from the beginning. The first — at first the more visible — was its striving for greater tactical militancy than NAWSA went in for, such as picketing; though in fact its tactics never reached the level of militancy of the British suffragists who had inspired its leaders. This difference faded in importance after the vote was achieved in 1920.

The second distinctive characteristic pointed to its future: from the beginning it believed in being a one-issue organization. Up to 1920 this meant concentration on the single issue of the suffrage amendment. After the 1920 victory, the N.W.P. had to reorient; it had to find another single issue to concentrate on; and in this period the deeper meaning of its type of concentration became more visible. *It was a way of saying that these women were not interested in anything else.*

What was "anything else"? The great leaders of the women's movement, then and previously, had by and large been social progressives at the least, and social radicals at the best. To be sure, they understood these things in different ways, practiced them to different degrees, and exercised more or less consistency in application. Such differentiation was inevitable. But it remained for the founders of the National Woman's Party to invent a new kind of feminism. This kind of feminism abstracted *from all other social concerns* a concern only with an abstract statement of equal rights, abstractly formulated.

This abstraction, or what formally looked like an abstraction, had a concrete social content, like everything else in the real world. It is not a matter of psychoanalyzing the motivations of the N.W.P.'s moving spirit, Alice Paul — an intense type for whom the one-issue approach may indeed have been an ideological abstraction. The approach which she presided over spoke loudly of its social content, not necessarily because of Alice Paul but despite her abstractionism.

The pattern was symbolized by the ascendancy to the presidency of the organization by its bankroller, Mrs. O. H. P. Belmont, the blue-blood socialite, who liked to orate that "henceforth women are to be dictators" and to predict portentously that the N.W.P. would soon "be strong enough to impose any measure it may choose."[8] It was a thin upper crust of women (and those who aspired to make it up there) who could afford to be uninterested in "anything else," that is, to ignore the social conditions of the mass of workingwomen. In practice, this approach meant counterposing abstract "women's rights" to concrete women's conditions.

All this was acted out when the feminists had to turn from the suffrage victory to the question of what to do next. The social-feminists had plenty to do. They went to work for a number of causes: independent citizenship for women, particular abuses in women's rights, the first federal venture into social-welfare legislation (the Maternity and Infancy Protection Act), consumer legislation, conservation, and many other social-reform and good-government issues, of more or less interest to women as such.

The N.W.P., on the other hand, as a one-big-blast organization, had to devise a "pure" single-shot issue to replace the vote. Its choice was still another constitutional amendment, carpentered as a general statement of "equal rights." This Equal

Rights Amendment was launched at a Washington convention in early 1921, and formalized in 1923.*

The implications of the N.W.P.'s new single-shooter were immediately apparent to both kinds of feminists. Lemons summarizes the immediate outcome as follows:

> The National Woman's Party was quite alone in 1923 with its amendment, but began picking up support in the late twenties, especially among business and professional women. After the buffeting which social feminism took over the child labor amendment [because of its defeat] and as professional concerns increased among women, a growing number turned from social issues to questions of personal interest. The equal rights amendment provided a pole toward which business and professional women gradually moved in the 1920s; and the 1930s saw a substantial number of the business and professional women's associations endorse the Woman's Party amendment.[9]

In other words, to use a term popular among the social-feminists, the N.W.P. took on the role of a "vanguard" organization for middle-class feminists. It never sought mass numbers; and in this sense did not really pretend to be a "party" in any popular sense. Its self-orientation was that of an elite. It could and did boast of Very Important Women: women who had made it in the

---

* When the E.R.A. was first introduced in Congress, its essential sentence read: "Men and women shall have equal rights throughout the United States and every place subject to its jurisdiction." From May 1943 on, the one-sentence formula went as follows: "Equality of rights under the law shall not be denied or abridged by the United States or by any State on account of sex."

arts and letters; tycoons' wives, like Mrs. William Randolph Hearst and the wife of General Motors' president; Pearl Mesta and Gloria Swanson; presidents and deans of women's colleges; a couple of presidents of the National Federation of Business and Professional Women's Clubs; and so on.

Such an organization would not have been well equipped without a token trade-unionist or two. The woman whom Alice Paul especially recruited to play this part was Maud Younger of San Francisco, who qualified for her N.W.P. role by helping to organize a waitresses union in the first decade of the century and then playing a leading role in the movement for an eight-hour day for women. Younger, wrote Alice Paul in her memoirs, was the N.W.P.'s "leading woman ... in the women's trade-union movement. ... Everything to do with labor, we always turned over to her." Recruited in 1915, Younger remained with Paul to become one of her hatchet-wielders to destroy the kind of legislation which had gained her the confidence of the trade-union women to whom she now offered the one-sentence amendment as the new salvation.[10] Florence Kelley, her friend and former colleague, wrote her in the early 1920s that sadly "your present activity runs counter to my continuous efforts of more than five and thirty years,"[11] but politely refrained from saying that it also ran counter to whatever had earned Younger the friendship of great souls like Kelley. Alice Paul's memoirs did not indicate how Younger explained her apostasy, or *if* she did, but she was hardly the first defector in the ranks of labor.

3 Two Women: Florence Kelley and Alice Paul

Then, as now, there *were* many gender-based injustices and anti-women discriminations that the proposed Equal Rights Amendment might have helped eliminate or reduce. The social-feminists could not fail to feel the attraction of such an amendment. They were for equal rights, and if an amendment could make an approach to equality, then it could be a good thing (quite apart from the strategic question of concentrating the whole movement on it).

At first some of them thought that the obvious impact of the Amendment in destroying labor legislation for women was only a matter of bad formulation. The National Woman's Party itself began by being unclear about this, at least entertaining the possibility of a reformulation that would not have such a catastrophic effect. Perhaps its leader had not begun by thinking the issue through. But quite soon the N.W.P. came out officially with what turned out to be its permanent line: the destruction of labor legislation for workingwomen was not an undesired by-product of the Amendment; it was one of the basic aims of the Amendment itself. "Special protective legislation" for women was evil, and had to be rooted out.

Florence Kelley was one of the members of the National Council of the N.W.P.; she had been attracted to the organization on the militancy issue. She was one of those who began by believing that an agreement could be reached between the social-feminists and the Paulites that would allow the whole movement to advocate *an* equal rights amendment. We need not take the space to describe her serious efforts to reach an agree-ment; they ended when she realized (or, quite possibly, when Alice Paul realized) that the N.W.P. had declared war-on-principle against the women's social legislation to which she, Kelley, had been devoting a large part of her life.

Mary Anderson, the Women's Bureau head who had grown up as a dedicated trade-unionist, also pondered the Amendment for some weeks before concluding that no alternative wording could be devised to preserve labor legislation. The conclusion for Anderson, Kelley, and others like them, was that there was no possibility of drafting a suitable text acceptable to the N.W.P. that would spare workingwomen's gains. Kelley spoke out her opinion that a blanket equality decree of the one-blast type would do more harm than good; she broke with the N.W.P., and became one of the leading opponents of the E.R.A.

Kelley's whole career, her whole life, explains why she had to come to this conclusion. That career and that life characterize one of the greatest leaders of the women's movement in this country. Her commitment to progressive social change began very early.

Born in 1859, she came from a well-to-do, socially conscious Quaker family in Philadelphia. As she later wrote: "Free Soilers and Revolutionary ancestors, Quakers and Abolitionists and Non-Conformists, family figures who had put their consciences to the tests both of endurance and action. Such [was] ... the heritage of one Philadelphia child of sixty years ago."[1] Her father, a Republican Congressman, actively supported women's suffrage, opposed slavery, and condemned the newly developed ills of an industrial society. Childhood memories of accompanying her father on factory tours ("a living horror") remained with her all through life. And she often recalled the philosophical directive her father had emphasized:

> That the duty of his generation was to build up
> great industries in America so that wealth could
> be produced for the whole people. "The duty of
> your generation," he often said, "will be to see

that the product is distributed justly. The same generation cannot do both."

Florence Kelley can be seen as the very model of the generous-hearted middle-class liberal that this country produced in quantity in its progressive era; but she was also different. She went farther than liberalism.

After graduating with a B.A. degree from Cornell in 1882, she was denied admission to graduate school at the University of Pennsylvania, which still refused to matriculate women. She went to Europe, therefore, and began graduate work in Zurich in 1883. It was there that she first heard a lecture on "The Program of the Social Democracy" given by the exiled German socialist leader Eduard Bernstein (then still in his leftist phase). The discussion that followed his remarks greatly excited Kelley, and (as she tells us) she took an "eager plunge into the enthusiasm of the new movement..." She joined up as a socialist while still in Zurich, and never gave up her socialist convictions.

Through the winter of 1883–1884 she read much Social-Democratic writing, including works by Marx and Engels. Eager to make a concrete contribution to the movement in English, Kelley made arrangements with Engels to translate his forty-year-old work *The Condition of the Working Class in England in 1844,* and her translation, revised by the author, was in fact published in 1887.

While still living in Europe, she fell in love with a Russian socialist exile, Lazare Wischnewetsky; they were soon married, and returned together to the United States. (Until her divorce she used the name Mrs. Florence K. Wischnewetsky; after divorce she returned to the name Florence Kelley, under which her great subsequent career is best known.) In the United States the

Wischnewetskys joined the only socialist organization then existing, the Socialist Labor Party — which, as she personally knew — her friend Engels regarded as a disaster for socialism; and indeed both Wischnewetskys were expelled in 1887 for opposition to the incredibly sectarian and hidebound leadership of this peculiar organization. Later Kelley joined the Socialist Party, and was active in the Intercollegiate Socialist Society for a number of years; but her main activity was carried on in more broadly based organizations involving immediate reforms. It was through this work that she made a lasting impact on the lives of workingpeople in America.

During the 1890s Kelley lived and worked at Jane Addams' famous settlement house (plus social and political center), Hull House, in Chicago. Here she directed a landmark survey of slum conditions on the city's West Side. The survey results helped Kelley's next fight: ending the widespread practice of industrial homework, or "sweating," a system in which thousands of men, women and children toiled under the worst possible conditions. Her efforts, in coalition with organized labor in the state, led to the passage of Illinois's first Factory Labor Law, in 1893. The act prohibited child labor, shortened the work-day for women and teen-age workers, set health and safety standards for industrial working conditions, and allowed the state to oversee enforcement of the law through factory inspection.

These appreciable gains for the worst-exploited victims of the sweatshops she later had to defend against the strictures of middle-class feminists — middle-class not because of their personal origins but because of their mental inability to see the real social world through the eyes of the victims of the system, rather than its upper crust. Kelley tried to explain why these victims could not protect their interests through trade-unionism alone:

> The vast majority of women wage-earners are between the ages of 16 and 25 years. They are not the material of which militant trade unions are formed. Their wages are too small to supply war chests for strikes. Their accumulated experience is too slight for the successful conduct of more than an occasional brief walkout. These facts common to all industrial countries compel protective legislation for women.[2]

Kelley herself served as Illinois's first Chief Factory Inspector under this law. When a conservative governor took office a few years later, she lost this position.

In 1899 she moved to New York City, where she took on the job she would have for the rest of her active life: general secretary of the National Consumers League. Middle-class women had organized this league to assist department store clerks, largely women, to improve their working conditions, using the weapon of consumer boycotts. Trade unions had not succeeded in this field (as yet); this is a good example of how workingpeople (specifically, mostly workingwomen) got an important assist from middle-class well-wishers. The N.C.L.'s constitution stated that its aim was to "educate public opinion and to endeavor so to direct its force as to promote better conditions among the workers, while securing to the consumer exemption from the dangers attending unwelcome conditions."[3]

Using the N.C.L. as her base, Kelley participated in dozens of battles for social progress over the next three decades. She led efforts to shorten the work-day, to set a minimum wage, to end child labor and the industrial homework system, to improve health and safety on the job, and to urge passage of a comprehensive federal bill for infant and maternity care (the issue which Professor Sylvia Hewlett had to painfully rediscover for herself). We have already mentioned her activity in favor of women's suffrage, first as vice-president of N.A.W.S.A., then as a national leader (temporarily) of the more militant N.W.P., and always as an independent woman.

For Kelley, obviously, the suffrage victory left no gap that had to be filled by inventing another issue; there were a large number of battles still to be won. On first hearing of the N.W.P.'s proposal for the one-blast Amendment, Kelley, like other social-feminist leaders, made an attempt to reach a compromise to save women's legislative gains. According to Josephine Goldmark, Kelley's coworker in the National Consumers League and later her biographer,

> On December 4, 1921, Mrs. Kelley, for the
> National Consumers League; Miss Ethel Smith,
> for the National Women's Trade Union League;
> Miss Maud Wood Park, for the National League
> of Women Voters; and representatives of the
> General Federation of Women's Clubs and of the
> Young Women's Christian Association met for
> two hours with Miss [Alice] Paul and two
> members of the board of the [National] Woman's
> Party, but to no effect.[4]

This sentence sums up the battle lines between the most active organizations of the women's movement, on the one hand, and on the other, the "topsy-turvy feminism" of the new group. (The term was Kelley's.)

The representative of "topsy-turvy feminism" in this lineup, Alice Paul, came from a background that was superficially much like Kelley's, but differed precisely with respect to preparation for social issues. Both were of middle-class origin, to be sure, but the immense difference was in how they viewed the world around them.

Alice Paul was twenty-six years younger than Kelley, born in 1885. She also came from a well-to-do Pennsylvania Quaker family, her father a successful banker. Her upbringing stressed the importance of education and an independent career, but provided no serious introduction to social questions. While she soon learned to be a sophisticated political organizer, her approach to social issues was rather simplistic. This is what she herself recalled later, in oral memoirs:

> First of all, I never heard of the idea of anybody being *opposed* to the idea [of suffrage or equality]; I just knew women didn't vote. I know my father believed and my mother believed in and supported the suffrage movement, and I remember my mother taking me to suffrage meetings.... It was just — I just never thought about there being any problem about it. It was the one thing that had to be *done,* I guess that's how I thought.[5]

She graduated from Swarthmore College in 1905, did some graduate work at the Columbia School of Social Work (then known as the School of Philanthropy), and went on to receive a

Ph.D. from the University of Pennsylvania, which was no longer refusing to admit women as it had done in Florence Kelley's day. Alice Paul wrote her doctoral thesis on women and equality, completing it in 1912.

Before completing the doctorate, however, she took time off to travel to Britain. It was there that she began working for women's suffrage. After seeing Christabel Pankhurst shouted down at a British university, Alice Paul was moved to join the movement. She later recalled her motivation as follows:

> ... I just became from that moment very anxious to help in this movement. You know if you feel some group that's your group is the underdog you want to try to help; it's natural I guess for everybody.

She joined the British Women's Social and Political Union, spoke at public meetings, sold its paper *Votes for Women,* marched in demonstrations, and was arrested more than once during protest "deputations" to Parliament and in other rallies.

On returning to the United States, she first joined N.A.W.S.A., the main suffrage organization, rising quickly in its leadership. In 1914 she split off from N.A.W.S.A. to form the Congressional Union, and, as we have seen, this evolved into the National Woman's Party in 1916.

When the N.W.P. adopted the one-blast Amendment as its end-all and be-all, Alice Paul remained true to her pattern of unconcern about splitting the movement to carry out her ideas. To a minor extent the first split was in her own organization; opposition to and suspicion of the Amendment were not limited to Florence Kelley in the N.W.P. But it was conceived not as a mass organization in the first place, but as an elite "ginger group," and the loss of a few members was not important. She was not much affected one way or the other by the divisive effect of the E.R.A. strategy. When she looked back to this period in her oral memoirs, she tried to make this clear to her interviewer:

Fry: Was the equal rights concept then looked upon as a unifying concept of all these diverse interest groups?

Paul:No.

Fry: It wasn't seen as some symbol of women's equality like suffrage had been?

Paul: Well, you see we never thought that there was any great mass of people in the country that wanted equality. We knew *we* wanted equality.

Fry:Who's we?

Paul:We of the Woman's Party wanted equality.

What the interviewer found it a little difficult to understand was that Alice Paul had succeeded, in her own mind, in acquiring her very *own* issue; or, more accurately, her very own group's issue...

In 1921 the N.W.P. held a convention in Washington at which women's organizations were invited to offer their proposals to the "Woman's Party" for action; but in fact Alice Paul and her associates had already made up their minds.[6] It is interesting to see how in her oral memoirs she recalls the contributions of women's leaders with social concerns, specific-ally Jane Addams and the well-known social-feminist leader Crystal Eastman. It was all a blur to her:

At the convention I remember Miss Jane Addams get-ting up and from the floor saying, "I hope you will all decide to join with the Women's International League for Peace and Freedom, make that your future." And Crystal Eastman went with a very involved feminist program... But it was — well, we didn't give a second thought to it. It was more embracing everything that Russia was doing and taking in all kinds of things we didn't expect to take in at all.

For the same reason it is worth quoting her recollection of her conflict with Florence Kelley, though it takes a bit more space and the blur is stronger:

Oh, that was an enormous, *enormous* campaign to get us to go into the field that the Consumers League, with Florence Kelley, was into. That was *tremendous* because so many of our women had helped put through these special labor laws for women.... [Kelley] was one of our strong members in the suffrage campaign. She was a leader in the campaign and had a meeting in Washington to which she invited *all* women's organizations to try to get them all to form a sort of coalition to work together for what the Consumers League was working for. She was one of the *strongest* people in trying to get this put in our program. Well, we kept saying, "But we stand for equality and your special labor laws are not in harmony with the principle that we're standing for." ... I remember these just bitter fights with the special-labor-laws-for-women people.

What this stream of consciousness accurately shows is how thoroughly abstract was Paul's approach to the issue. Neither here nor elsewhere was she capable of analyzing the concrete social meaning and consequences of the "labor-laws-for-women" business, including the workingwomen's conditions which she was out to break down. For the question was not posed this way in her mind. You are either for "equality" or you are not, and if you are for, you need only a few words to say so, and that's an end on't. Above all, it must not be supposed that Alice Paul wished any harm to come to workingwomen; she hardly could do so, since they scarcely existed in her mentality.

Alice Paul's abstract Equality was intended to be a *legal* abstraction. She explained in her oral memoirs:

> [The E.R.A.] is only a prohibition on the *government* of the country. An individual family, such as you and your husband, can have inequality with you the head of the family or he the head of the family or anything you want to do.... I think as far as law and government, the Amendment won't do away with all the innumerable phases of the subjection of women...

She herself took a roseate view of women's traditional role in society, having swallowed some of the sexist illusions that made the early suffragist movement claim that women's voting would revolutionize the political scene by itself.

> I think men contribute one thing and women
> another thing, that we're made that way. Women
> are made as the peaceloving half of the world and
> the home-making half of the world, the temperate
> half of the world. The more power they have, the
> better world we are going to have...

The reason for this benign outcome, she thought, was that
women are by nature "raisers of children" and "want to make it
the best possible home." Furthermore, "you have a force that's
not thinking all the time about going out and fighting somebody
in the economic struggle or in any other struggle." If a man were
to utter these hallowed sentiments, he would be *rightly* accused
of claiming that women's place (or at least her best place) was in
the home, and at any rate outside of "the economic struggle."

Thus the abstract proponent of abstract women's "equality"
turns out to hold the same presuppositions about "women" as the
typical men of her day. We would remind that in *A Lesser Life*
Professor Sylvia Hewlett now demonstrates a somewhat similar
pattern at work when she shows how the E.R.A.-feminism of the
'70s and '80s produces the model of the "male-clone" as the
"liberated woman"...[7]

4 Wisconsin Demonstrates the E.R.A.

In 1921–1922, while the split was hardening between the social-feminist majority of the women's movement and the Paulite offshoot (National Woman's Party), the first Equal Rights Amendment of any kind was established in the state of Wisconsin. Its history is a brilliantly illuminated comment on the pattern that was going to be acted out during the subsequent history of the national E.R.A. question.

This story may be summarized as follows: (1) The Wisconsin law was an E.R.A. that could be and was supported by the social-feminists and workingwomen's advocates, that is, a "workingwomen's E.R.A." (2) Insofar as it was allowed to work out, it showed none of the disastrous effects on women's independence that the Paulites predicted; on the contrary it was an unquestionably positive measure for all women's interests. (3) It was obstructed by the same united front we will see at work in the next chapter, the abstract feminists of the Pure amendment plus the traditionalist right of the Establishment.

The Wisconsin law was not, in origin, the outcome of agitation by the women's movement. The law (says Lemons)

> ... grew out of a general desire to clarify women's rights after the Nineteenth Amendment and from politicians' hopes of capturing the women's vote. Governor John J. Blair had been elected on a platform promising equality.[1]

Like many other states, Wisconsin in the first part of the twentieth century had adopted a number of labor laws for women workers, passed under the combined pressure of women's groups, social welfare organizations, and the trade-union movement.

For example, in January 1917 a "Petition and Statement of Facts" was submitted jointly by the Wisconsin Federation of Labor, the Milwaukee Council of Social Agencies, and the Wisconsin Consumers League, and sent to the Wisconsin Industrial Commission, in support of a proposal for reduced working hours for women. These organizations presented a detailed survey comparing the working hours of men and women, concluding that "It will thus be seen that, in 1915, 17,609 union men worked less time than the hours fixed by law for women, per week, and only 5,533 worked as many or more hours than fixed by law for women."[2] Any enterprise affecting women workers had to take these forces into account. It must also be remembered that there was a strong socialist movement around Milwaukee: Victor Berger had been elected as the first socialist congressman from that area, first in 1911 and again in 1918 and 1919 (only to be illegally thrown out of Congress in the wartime and postwar anti-Red hysteria) and later served from 1923 on, at a time when Milwaukee also began electing socialist mayors. The N.W.P.'s state chair, Mabel Putnam, was active in leading the movement, but her organization's policy was still in flux; and recognizing that the N.W.P. by itself was not strong enough to carry the equal-rights proposal, she sought the support of other groups. The final wording of the Wisconsin E.R.A. stated that its purpose was "to remove discrimination against women and to give them equal rights before the law.... The statutes where the masculine gender is used [are] to include the feminine gender *unless such construction will deny to females the special protection and privileges which they now enjoy for the general welfare..."* [Emphasis added to original.][3]

With this provision allowing room for labor legislation applying to women only, the sponsors obtained the support of the important women's organizations, such as the Women's Progressive Association of the La Follette movement, part of the League of Women Voters, the State Federation of Women's Clubs, the Wisconsin Council of Catholic Women, the Wisconsin Consumers League, the Y.W.C.A., the Socialist Party, and others. How heartening this new unity was may be seen from the enthusiastic words of Mabel Putnam herself, published not much later:

> Such a different-minded group of women gathered together in common support of one bill; women representing organizations, some of them, which were even working for causes in opposition! But women who all put the emancipation of women above every other cause. Other differences did not count, in the face of the tremendous importance of winning full citizenship for women.[4]

This was the first and last time that such a broad front to expand women's rights and interests, comprising even the Paulites of the National Woman's Party, could be achieved. The N.W.P.'s increasingly adamant refusal to allow labor legislation for women in its national E.R.A. would prevent such a concentration of strength ever again.

The situation in Wisconsin, even with an E.R.A. formulation that exempted special women's gains, showed that there was a certain suspicion of a blanket approach to women's rights. The League of Women Voters was a case in point.

Initially the state organization of the League had testified in favor of the proposal; but later the Milwaukee branch pulled back from it, in favor of a "specific bills for specific ills" approach only. The Milwaukee people asserted they wanted to support only the right to jury service, since this was closely related to voting rights. The League's statewide vice-president, however, continued to speak for the full bill. It may well be that, even at this early point, the League people (no radicals they) were fearful of the effect of any blanket statement on "specific bills for specific ills." Certainly, later on when the League was vigorously opposing the Paulites' national E.R.A. (the "pure" E.R.A.), their leaders made this point. Esther Dunshee, their spokesperson on the issue, emphasized that the advocates of the "pure" thing wanted to destroy "all protective legislation affecting only women" and held the view that this destruction is a desirable thing. "But statistics show," Dunshee wrote, "that such protection is warranted... the best results can only be obtained by a carefully worked-out system of laws, not by hasty, ill-considered blanket legislation."[5]

But, back in Wisconsin, Mabel Putnam — not yet straightened out by Alice Paul — was "delighted" with the language of the bill, which had been worked on by the state legislature's own staff; it was "a marvel of simplicity and completeness." She called on the governor, who, she said, "agreed with the last section of the bill that the law relating to labor, as it affects women, should not be affected by a general act abolishing other discriminations."[6]

The movement behind the Wisconsin E.R.A. effectively faced only the strong opposition of the traditionalists of the right, such as the state assemblyman Alexander E. Matheson. His argument was the familiar one:

> There are three pillars of state — religion, education, and the home, and of these the home is the greatest of all. In the home the mother is the center. Our civil-ization is tottering and crumbling and I think we should go slow in passing legislation of this kind. This bill will result in coarsening the fiber of woman — it takes her out of her proper sphere.[7]

The new law passed easily in the Legislature, and was signed into law by the governor in July 1921.

Later that year, a "Wisconsin Women's Committee on Study of [the 1921]...Women's Equal Rights Law" was set up as the result of a resolution adopted by the annual convention of the Wisconsin Federation of Women's Clubs. Because of all of the free-floating predictions about the horrible (or for that matter beneficent) consequences of the new law, the aim was to investigate what its effects *had* been in fact. A number of women's organizations added representatives to this committee: the American Association of University Women, the Women's Progressive Association (La Follette), Consumers League, League of Women Voters, Women's Trade Union League, and others. The investigation was conducted by Irma Hochstein, of the state's Legislative Reference Library, through 1922, until September when the committee report was issued.

This report is a unique historical document, the only *factual* response to the myriad of predictions and guesses and charges that had been flung about, and *that were going to be flung about on the national scene, by the proponents of a "pure" E.R.A., against a workingwomen's version of an E.R.A.* This one and only example of a workingwomen's E.R.A. had been in force for a year and two months when the report came out, and there was never going to be such an opportunity again.

The report offered both general summary statements and specific, detailed accounts of real cases and situations. Here is a summary statement:

> During that time [the year and two months] no instance of injustice to women under the law had occurred. Numerous illustrations show that the law has worked for a greater degree of justice and greater equality of women with men than they had before the passage of the law.

Example: The committee pointed out that the Milwaukee City Civil Services Commission had considered, under the pressure of an unemployment crisis, "adoption of a rule limiting the employment of married women both by excluding them in the notice of examination and providing for dismissal of married women in the service." But under the new state E.R.A. the commission was debarred from imposing this rule.

Example: Up to now all efforts to increase the number of women on Milwaukee's police force had run up against the force's prohibition of married women. This barrier was now broken down by the state E.R.A.

Example: Married women could now establish a legal place of residence independent of their husbands; and "throughout the state women are serving on juries" now.[8]

Example: Women's employment situation improved relatively. Employment statistics by sex, though hard to come by, indicate (as far as they exist) that the law had a positive influence in the years after its passage. As recorded by the Wisconsin

Industrial Commission: in the year ending June 30, 1923, Public Employment Offices reported placing 130,978 persons in new jobs, women constituting 21.1%. At the end of 1925, the number placed in the previous year had dropped to 105,704, but now 25.7% were women. It must be remembered that a drop in employment traditionally meant that an *increased* proportion of the change was borne by women; even the maintenance of a given percentage would have been an improvement, let alone this recorded rise. A year and a half later, the Commission reported another decline to 97,344 persons placed in the preceding year, yet the women's percentage remained constant at 25.7%.[9]

The pessimists' prediction that the new law would cause the courts to be jammed with lawsuits demanding interpretation was not borne out, any more than the traditionalists' forecasts that the social order and the family would self-destruct in short order. During about a dozen years after the passage of the state E.R.A., the state Supreme Court upheld it in case after case. And subsequent reports by the state Legislative Reference Library upheld the conclusions of the Wisconsin Women's Committee of September 1922.[10]

We have mentioned that there was an initial period before Alice Paul and her National Woman's Party hardened their position on the "pure" E.R.A. and suppressed all possibility of compromise with the social-feminists. In this interim the group expressed delight with the passage of the Wisconsin law. Mabel Putnam later quoted Alice Paul as writing in a party news bulletin that "This makes Wisconsin the only spot in the United States where women have, or have ever had since the beginning of our country, full equality with men..."[11]

But as the Paulites' national position on a Pure E.R.A. began to harden through 1921 and 1922, what had been hailed as a "Bill of Rights for the women of Wisconsin" was transformed into an example of what not to do. How this flip-flop was achieved provides a good example of how the N.W.P. approached politics. What happened was that the group seized on a bad ruling made by Wisconsin's attorney general, Herman L. Ekern, in early 1923.

A ruling by one politician was enough to turn two years of experience topsy-turvy? The answer is, of course, that it gave the Paulites the only pretext they had available. It was not even a good pretext, if we examine what happened.

Ekern's ruling was that a 1905 state law prohibiting the employment of women as clerks and aides in the state Legislature was *consistent* with the new E.R.A. He based this decision on the argument that such "employees must devote to the service long hours and often be on duty at very unseasonable hours." He claimed that the ruling "did not spring from any desire to exclude women from employment but from a desire for the protection of women against the conditions and requirements of such employment." (So he wrote in a letter sent to the N.W.P.)[12]

The attorney general's ruling was very vulnerable (not many people would consider a legislative clerkship as a position detrimental to morals), and a united movement had a plain road to overthrowing it in the courts. Besides, Ekern himself pointed out that it would be "a simple matter to meet the question if the legislature may find at any time that it is desirable to specifically change this rule."[13] And so the Legislature itself could invalidate the new ruling — by finding that its *own* women clerks were not in danger of losing their immortal souls or social innocence. In fact, the attorney general's ruling was a pretty feeble attempt to sabotage the state E.R.A.

But by this time the N.W.P. did not need a strong pretext; it could not continue to support the Wisconsin E.R.A. and at the same time break nationally with the majority of the women's movement over the Pure E.R.A. Instead of solidifying the Wisconsin law by campaigning for a rebuke to Ekern by either the courts or the Legislature, it became part of the front to destroy the new law — for its own reasons, of course.

The Paulites now claimed that the clause exempting women's labor laws was instrumental in excluding women from jobs, for wasn't this the clause that Ekern had fastened onto? Instead of a "Bill of Rights" for women, the law was now

> An example of the working out in practice of laws purporting to give special privileges to women... Nothing could show more vividly what "privileges" and what "protection" really mean to women. Nothing, moreover, could show more clearly the wisdom of the Woman's Party ... in opposing the so-called "safeguarding" clauses such as that contained in the Wisconsin law, which assume to give "protection" and "privilege" to women...[14]

The N.W.P. launched campaigns in other states for a statewide E.R.A. — a Pure E.R.A. — but now this was not only a one-blast amendment, it was a one-group slogan property. No cooperation with the social-feminists was possible; and this in fact meant no cooperation with any other women's organization of any consequence. The Wisconsin "workingwomen's E.R.A."

was the only blanket law for equal rights ever adopted during the next several decades.

We can say with a certain amount of confidence that, if the women's movement had remained united in support of the Wisconsin E.R.A., that experiment could well have been the first step of a national drive for a similar E.R.A. It is quite possible that we could have had *an* equal rights amendment in this country decades before the fiasco-E.R.A. of the '70s and '80s. But it would have had to be a workingwomen's E.R.A., not the Pure thing, and the National Woman's Party made sure that it did not happen. By the end of this episode, the N.W.P. policy amounted to rule-or-ruin: either we get the Pure amendment in all its purity, or else we wreck every effort to win an E.R.A. favorable to workingwomen. If the reader believes this is an exaggeration, in a little while we will read Alice Paul's own description of her wrecking-crew approach.

5 The Investigation: Facts Versus Claims

Out of the shambles of the Second Conference on Women in Industry came one positive result.

Since the N.W.P. had hardened its position on rejecting all labor legislation for women on principle, it had begun developing a number of claims purporting to strengthen its view. One claim was that tens and hundreds of thousands of women had lost their jobs because of such legislation. (Proof: Gladys Smith had lost her job at Brown & Jones... etc.) One of the N.W.P. leaders gave out the figure of 150,000 women in New York State alone; another dropped the first digit of this figure when testifying before a Senate Committee; but a survey by the Women's Bureau of the claimed situations turned up only 149 ticket sellers and eight printers. Anyone with experience with labor legislation in general would understand that *every* piece of such legislation has a minimum shakeout effect, which has to be reviewed for ad-hoc injustices and remedied. It was the imaginative size of its claimed figures that the N.W.P. relied on for effect.

Mary Anderson of the Women's Bureau made sure that the Second Conference mandated such an investigation; the difficulty was that so many of the women there were so incensed against the N.W.P. that they were reluctant to vote for anything that might appear to be a concession to the disrupters.

The investigation into the effects of special labor legislation for women was carried out, and it was the most extensive and expensive inquiry ever conducted by the Women's Bureau, using the entire staff and the money provided by two years' worth of appropriations. The facts were laid out in the report published in 1928. Following is a summary.[1]

Covered were eleven states, with reports "secured from more than 1,600 establishments, employing more than 660,000 men and women, and personal interviews were held with more than 1,200 working women who had experienced a change in the law or who were employed under conditions or in occupations prohibited for women in some other State." The facts thus presented constituted a crushing refutation of the claims made by the Pure E.R.A. proponents about the alleged harmful effects of the legislation being investigated.

There was a telltale controversy at the beginning of the inquiry that both sides agreed was necessary. To ensure objectivity throughout, the Women's Bureau suggested that two advisory committees be formed: one technical in nature, "composed of persons having experience in carrying forward industrial investigations"; the second, made up of representatives from organizations on both sides of the dispute. Right off, however, the N.W.P. representatives on this second committee argued *against* the length and detailed investigation proposed by the Women's Bureau. *The Party stalwarts "urged that the investigation be conducted from the beginning mainly from public hearings."* (Our emphasis added.)

The meaning of this proposal was clear. If the "facts" were to be sought through a parade of witnesses each claiming whatever he or she felt like claiming, the Pure forces could get as many such testifiers to march through the hearing room as anyone else. In fact this was, in effect, precisely what had been happening up to now: everyone making whatever claim seem-ed impressive, with no way of checking on anyone. But this "public hearing" format was much more the style of the N.W.P. than of the social-feminists. The N.W.P. could (and would) parade movie stars like Gloria Swanson to testify from *her* expert knowledge of labor legislation, and the newspaper headlines would bury the six-point references to Florence Kelley. After all, besides its activists the N.W.P. was systematically *composed* of elite names — prominent socialites, wives and daughters of politicians, celebrities like the daughters of William Jennings Bryan, and so on. An "investigation" of the sort proposed by the Paulites would be a farce, scientifically speaking, but it would be a high-circulation farce from the press's standpoint and a media-jubilee from the standpoint of the Pure amendment. At the end, to be sure, no one would know any more than at the start about the factual effects of labor legislation — but *who* exactly wanted to know, anyhow?

The Women's Bureau did not comment on the scheme in the way done here. It merely objected that the process proposed by the N.W.P. "could not be relied upon to bring out all the facts." The National Woman's Party people then moved to destroy this second advisory committee. In a campaign of pressure against Congressional representatives, they charged the Bureau with prejudice — before the study had even begun. That is, the Bureau was "prejudiced" because it had refused to accept their scheme to scuttle the investigation. The advisory committee in question was then dissolved, but the study proceeded under the guidance of the technical committee.

The difference was this: it could no longer be said that the investigation was carried out under the superintendence of N.W.P. representatives themselves; the N.W.P. had made sure this couldn't be said, by torpedoing the proposed committee of superintendence.

The beginning of the report pointed out that the center of the investigation was not some special question about women but rather this:

> The validity and effectiveness of the legislative method of regulating and standardizing [working] conditions... Does legislation set up an arbitrary

standard at the expense of individual liberties? Where it applies only to limited groups of localities or persons, by curtailing individual freedom does it handicap such competitive efforts as are essential to curtail progress? Or does it, by establishing a minimum standard for some groups, raise the level for the whole so that competition may proceed on a fairer basis and higher plane?

The report moved on to discuss the historical context in which the controversy arose: the context was not declining opportunities for women to work, but just the opposite. A steady increase in employment for women outside the home and off the farm was registered from 1870 to 1920. At the start of this fifty-year span, some 11.8% of women were working, while at the close of the five decades the figure was 23.8%. In those industries that were most important in relation to labor legislation, manufacturing and mechanical industries, there was to be found a big jump in female employment, just from 1910. (A number of figures for given industries were detailed here.) "The most striking increase" was that of women operatives in auto factories: 1408%. In the entire iron and steel industry, women as semiskilled operatives increased over 145%; in electrical supply factories, over 148%. *These figures showed that the rates of increase/decrease for the two sexes had been "entirely disproportionate"* — in favor of women by far. "These huge in-creases ... indicate that more and more industrial opportunities are being offered to women."

The report did not go on to claim that women's improving employment status had been *due* to labor legislation; the two developments were going on side by side. What *did* it show? Women's place in industrial work was a fact. The advantages that such opportunities offered were to be welcomed. But the drawbacks entailed had to be dealt with, also: the Women's Bureau wished that women could continue working, and not be forced back out of the workplace because of intolerable hours, wages, and working conditions. Had labor legislation made *this* possible?

About the legal regulation of the hours that women might work, the report came to a clear conclusion:

> Not only have there been practically no instances of actual decreases in women's employment as a result of hour legislation, but the general status of their op-portunity seems not to have been limited by this type of law. Women were employed as extensively in California as in Indiana, in Massachusetts as in New York.

Indeed, because of the ceiling on hours of work, the Bureau found that more women were able to find employment than before because it was "not unusual for establishments to employ additional women when there is extra work or else to carry a larger force of women the year around..." (Let it be said parenthetically that that anecdotal story about a Gladys Smith still might be true enough; but the facts meant that such cases were individual cases, to be handled and remedied on an ad-hoc basis, like a thousand other anecdotal problems.)

Similar conclusions were reached from the facts when other forms of regulatory legislation were examined. Laws mandating rest rooms, seating, or improved ventilation were not a serious handicap to women's employment, though difficult to investigate separately because of their close relation-ship to developing standards of efficient management.

The report did find some restrictions on women's legitimate economic opportunity and occupations where legal prohibitions against night work or against work in certain fields were in effect. In most situations the lost opportunities were either minimal or else absolutely necessary to the woman worker's health. Especially in the latter case, the Bureau argued, steps should be taken to extend the health and safety protections also to men. Where job opportunities were eliminated unnecessarily, the legislation should be more carefully drawn.

In short, whatever grievances were felt in this field could become the target of a separate campaign, without throwing everything else out. The Bureau was not arguing that everything was already ideal; far from it. It was pointing out that there was obviously a different road than that of total-destruct.

So much for the anecdotal statistics that had been so freely employed by the Paulites. The report pointed in another important direction. The real source of the lost opportunities to women was not the legal enactment of prohibitions on employment, but *the prevailing attitudes of the employers, and also of some part of the male workers.* (Reminder to the reader: remember the B.R.T. case, and the exposure of the employer's role in that affair...)[2] The report charged:

> Far more important, however, than any possible limitation of opportunity resulting from night-work legislation is the limitation of women's work at night that results from the general managerial policies of most employers of women.

> There are conspicuous examples of
> establishments where night work for women is
> enthusiastically indorsed by the management, but
> the more usual attitude is dis-approbation from
> the standpoint of industrial efficiency.

A similar attitudinal barrier (involving *employers'* attitudes) was found in specific occupations where opportunities for women were limited. The report agreed that restrictive laws for women's employment in pharmacy were a problem; but it *also* went on to point out that "as far as concerns the actual position of women pharmacists the removal of such legislation would have very little effect." It pointed to two reasons here: the employers' attitudes and those of the public in dealing prejudicially with male and female pharmacists.

Employers' attitudes were also a target of the report with respect to work in restaurants and as elevator operators. The report concluded that

> In almost every kind of employment the real
> forces that influence women's opportunity are far
> removed from legislative restrictions of their
> hours or conditions of work.

It would be useful, though space-consuming, to cite the passages in which the report tried to emphasize that the question of legislative restrictions, no matter how important one thinks it is, is only one of several factors affecting women's employment. The report's emphasis on the employers' role is heavy, as mentioned; but no less significant is its stress on the role of an enlightened or unenlightened public and the public's acceptance or rejection of women in certain jobs. Obviously, here it was saying that the job was that of influencing public opinion — which also brings the employers right back in again. *In contrast, the N.W.P.'s favorite mode of approach let the employers off scot-free,* even though employers like to talk as if the jobs were "theirs." The formal alliance between the N.W.P. and the National Association of Manufacturers was a good deal for the latter; all the N.A.M. paid was lip-service to a constitutional amendment which (most lawyers were ready to explain) meant little in practice.

The report answered some other important questions.

(1) We have seen the answer with respect to employment; how about effect on wage level? The report replied that "the legal reduction of women's hours had not resulted in any general decrease" in workingwomen's wages. To be sure, some workingwomen might consider the advantage of a shorter work-day as less important than a slightly higher pay packet at the end of the week. But even among the small number of women reporting decreased wages as a result of shorter hours "three of every four definitely state[d] that the decrease in earnings was not looked on as a hardship in view of the benefits that accompanied shorter hours."

(2) The tendency has been for women's gains to be extended to men.

> There is no doubt that legislation limiting women's hours of work has reacted to establish shorter hour standards generally and to eliminate

isolated examples of long hours. Also, in a large majority of cases, when hours were shortened for women because of the law they were also shortened for men.

The Women's Bureau gave a number of examples, not only in this report but also in other bulletins.[3]

(3) The report examined the impact of legislatively determined work-hours limitations on the employment and promotion opportunities of women in supervisory capacities. Here, one of its findings was surprising to some: many women were reluctant to consider the promotions that were in fact open to them, "as they [the promotions] frequently involve a change from a wage based on production to a regular weekly wage, and some women are reluctant to give up the seemingly larger weekly amount they can earn through piecework." One of the elements here was a feeling of group solidarity or sense of class: "Other women sometimes are unwilling to undertake the duties of supervising the work of others as they are reluctant to assume a different relationship with their fellow workers."

But at the bottom of the problem was, here too, the reluctance of *the employers* to open up supervisory opportunities to women:

> Labor legislation does not hinder promotion, as there is practically no promotion to hinder.... [I]n comparison with the opportunity open to men for such work, women's opportunity is very slight and is dependent not on the limitations, legal or

otherwise, that surround women's work, but on the individual attitude of the employer and what he thinks is the attitude of their fellow workers.

Another important feature of the report was about a personal survey of over 900 women who worked in a variety of manufacturing and nonmanufacturing industries at the time when a shorter-hours law went into effect. What effects did the change have on an individual's "opportunity"? The women's comments were revealing.

"There was not one woman," the report stated, "who felt that legislation had handicapped her in getting work or promotion..." Quite the opposite! The interviews indicated that many of the women felt the shorter hours increased opportunity for themselves and women workers generally. A jewelry and optical-goods worker stressed that a woman could not work a 48-hour week "and get through her home duties," especially if she had a family to care for. A steel-plant inspector thought that opportunities for women have improved, "as it is [now] possible for more married women to work with shorter hours." A Massachusetts shoe worker ranged a little further in her interview with the investigator:

> I had rather work a short week. You get time to accomplish other things. Life is not all labor, and with shorter working hours, you may accomplish many things to broaden your mind. Money is not everything, it does not buy all. One who is confined to work can not broaden out and is narrow and unhappy.

The reader is invited to wonder how much of the Women's Bureau report on real workingwomen could be understood by the glamorous and celebrated women whom the N.W.P. liked to trot out in its publicity: women like Gloria Swanson or Mrs. O. H. P. Belmont or Bryan's daughters...

The report paid particular attention to the impact of labor laws on women employed in urban transit — the field that had given rise to the B.R.T. case. The situation in this industry best exemplified the Bureau's argument that *no wholesale conclusions* about protective legislative were possible apart from an examination of particular industries, localities, and political conditions. The report's findings were based on two earlier reports which examined seven different cities' transit systems and new research conducted by the Bureau in 1926.[4]

The report discussed a number of cases where women had suffered the loss of significant job opportunities or outright dismissal, and argued — as already indicated — that the determining factors were not legislative protections but the attitudes held by the employers and the male employees involved. Throwing the blame on the labor legislation was an employers' ploy to misdirect attention. In known cases where women employed as streetcar conductors lost their jobs, "the companies involved did not intend to keep them on permanently for this work" and the legislation perhaps accelerated their firings by providing them with a pretext. One way of testing what really happened was to compare the New York City pattern with other cities.

There were, the Bureau found, important differences among women transit workers from city to city. Women ticket agents and conductors faced a particularly difficult situation in New York. Though several hundred women were hired into the transit system during the war, these women *immediately* began losing their jobs when the Armistice was signed in November 1918. The regulatory law limiting work-hours came along several months later, in May 1919. Besides *limiting* hours (to nine a day, 54 a week, with no night work 10 p.m. to 6 a.m.), the New York law had a provision not found elsewhere: women's daily shifts had to be consecutive; that is, they could not work two rush hours with time off in between.

This last provision, the Bureau charged, was unnecessary to women's health, and allowed the transit companies to accelerate their dismissals of women workers. The Bureau could not *prove* that this out-of-line provision was there precisely to expedite the dismissals, but it said as much in the following words: "In the last analysis, the fact of the situation is that the policy of the company can not be divorced from the effects of certain kinds of laws." The obvious remedy was not to destroy the useful labor legislation but to make the legislation more "carefully drawn" by eliminating this provision of the New York law.

This point is underlined when, with the Bureau's report, we compare the New York case with that of other cities' labor legislation on women streetcar employees. In Boston and Chicago, the Bureau found in its 1921 study, "the 8-hour day and 6-day week, without night work, and with a wage far superior to that paid women in many other occupations ... is an accepted and permanent fact" for women ticket agents and conductors.

Similar conditions were found in Detroit and Kansas City. In Detroit, for example, "there was no evidence to show that women had been dismissed because of the difficulty of complying with the terms of the law."

What made the difference? This, said the report:

> Perhaps the most significant fact about the
> employment of women as ticket agents and
> collectors in [Boston and Chicago] is the way in
> which better hours and wages for them have been
> achieved. Women are members of the union in
> both Chicago and Boston, and it is with the
> assistance of the union that their hours have been
> shortened and their wages increased. In Chicago
> at the time when the 10-hour law for women was
> about to be passed in Illinois the union worked for
> this law, appearing before the legislature in favor
> of it, although its members were threatened with a
> reduction in pay. In subsequent strikes on the
> street railways the women have stood with the
> men in their efforts to improve conditions. The
> result in Chicago has been that conditions for
> women employed on the elevated railways are far
> ahead of the maximum legal requirement, and
> adjustments have been made, as in the elimination
> of night work for women, which can serve as an
> example to many other communities.[5]

Lemons summarizes the results of the 1928 report in very
positive terms.

> o Labor legislation was "not a handicap to
> women," and "did not reduce their opportunities."
> On the contrary, "it raised standards not only for
> women but for thousands of men too."

o It was not true that minimum-wage standards became the maximum; on the contrary, statistics showed clearly that workers so covered made higher pay than others on the average.

o On the whole, women were not handicapped by hours laws, though individual cases might be, and when women won these laws, men's hours tended to be shortened as well.

o The states that had the most advanced laws for women also had the greatest opportunities for women to work.

o Pacts showed that a body of protective legislation did not reduce the number of jobs but had the opposite results.

Most significantly, the Bureau found that the laws usually enforced upon the entire industry what the most advanced elements were already doing; in short, the laws tended to protect the most progressive tendencies in American business.[6]

The element in the situation that was constituted by male workers' prejudices *could* be counteracted by trade-unionism and conditions of common struggle, as we have seen in the case of the transit workers in several cities. But the main determinant of women's job opportunities was not labor legislation but rather *employers' conceptions* of what "women's jobs" were. In short, the main enemy was the N.W.P.'s ally, the gentlemen of the National Association of Manufacturers and the U.S. Chamber of

Commerce, who at this point were the only significant organizations supporting the N.W.P.'s symbol of equal rights, the Amendment designed to kill all social legislation for workingwomen in one fell swoop.

The report made clear that there *were* cases of women who were dismissed because of special laws. These cases could be reduced by careful drafting, or redrafting, of the laws; such changes had even been made already, as in 1919 among the printers. Nightwork regulations *had* caused a few women to lose jobs, but daytime opportunities had greatly increased. The report opposed the passage of any restrictive laws for hazardous jobs unless the hazard could be shown to be sex-related.

"The report," concludes Lemons, "effectively countered the NWP's factual arguments about protective legislation. All they had left was the ideological conviction that such laws promoted a sense of inferiority among women."[7] But this is what Alice Paul and her circle had *started* with.

This "argument" against labor legislation for women workers is still heard as often as ever, in the pages of *Ms* magazine and the statements of N.O.W. It is an argument of intense sociological interest. If a group of women workers are "granted" higher wages than men, they are urged by the N.W.P. types to *resent this largesse as patronizing;* but consider the entirely opposite kind of "psychology" among (say) trade-unionists. Any organized group of workers feel quite serene about winning higher wages than unorganized trades or shops; among other things, they know that the latter will be stimulated to win the raises (or conditions) for themselves. This is ABC in the labor movement, and even outside of it. As already mentioned, *women* trade-unionists feel no less content in conscience at making a gain for themselves, and turn some attention to extending the same gain to all others.

What then is this "psychology" of career-women (to use a conveniently vague term) that makes them look on a legislation victory as an "insult"? For one thing, it is very doubtful that the size of the "insult" will determine, for *these* women, what they can feed their families the next day... But this sociological investigation is not our present subject, and we willingly leave it to the reader's excogitation.

6 The "Right to Work" Ploy

One can see why the manufacturers' associations saw labor legislation for women as the entering wedge of a general social program that could cost them billions of dollars. But their propaganda efforts to save women from the indignity of better working conditions was considerably aided by a free gift to their position by the leaders of the then labor movement.

It has been mercifully forgotten by most people that for decades — up to the coming of the New Deal — the American Federation of Labor under Samuel Gompers was one of the most virulent opponents of social legislation for the protection of labor's interests. Minimum-wage laws were Gompers' special bugbear, and he did not support such laws even for women, though he let his guard down for shorter hours for women. Gompers' A.F.L. opposed social insurance — in the name of freedom.

> Sore and sad as I am [wrote Gompers in 1916] by the illness, the killing, the maiming of so many of my fellow workers, I would rather see that go on for years and years ... than give up one jot of the freedom of the workers to strive and struggle for their own emancipation through their own efforts.[1]

This lofty principle Gompers called *voluntarism,* and no selfstyled Libertarian of today could be more enthusiastic about denouncing "the State" than these labor leaders of the day who looked to labor-management collaboration as the answer to all social ills. It is not recorded that the workers who were sickened, maimed, or killed by their conditions of work were able to maintain the same staunch belief in Freedom.

The Gompers A.F.L. maintained that protective legislation (for men) would divert the attention of workers from their trade union organizations to political activity. The advocates of social legislation made people believe that law was a panacea for all ills. The A.F.L. convention of 1913 condemned a minimum-wage law because "Through organization, the wages of men can and will be maintained at a higher minimum than they would if fixed by legal enactment." Yes, but how about that large majority of America's workers who were *not* organized, and were not going to be organized very soon, either, if they depended on Gompers? (Keep your eye on this question, for it includes most women workers.)

The A.F.L. was violently opposed to the government's adopting a patriarchal attitude of concern for workers. The following pronouncement by Gompers is close in spirit to the business and professional women who claimed to be insulted and demeaned by protective legislation for women:

> That the state should provide sickness [insurance] for workers is fundamentally based upon the theory that these workmen are not able to look after their own interests and the state must interpose its authority and wisdom and assume the relation of parent or guardian.[2]

Gompers wound this up by hailing the "freeborn citizen." Modern E.R.A.-feminists would invoke their repugnance to the "male" assumption of mastery, presumably inherent in special protective laws for women. It is very, very easy today to see what was bothering Gompers.

The fact was that the labor aristocracy whom Gompers represented — the higher-paid skilled craft workers — did not need a minimum-wage law and would only have been embarrassed by it. When they argued that a minimum wage might be used to impose a maximum, they meant they wanted to protect *their* privileged position as against hoi polloi. *You see the pattern of a better-paid elite who are willing to make their advances by stepping on the recumbent backs of brother- and sister-workers.*

This was why the Gompers-A.F.L. argument against special protective laws *for men* sounds so much like the contemporary feminists' attack on special protective legislation for women. The only difference is that the former has been completely buried by history, and the latter is very much with us. But no one can formulate a critique of the Gompers-A.F.L. position that is not at the same time a refutation of the same theory as refurbished by N.O.W.

On the national scene, the drive for labor legislation — on a minimum wage, shorter hours, social insurance, etc. — was spearheaded *by the social-feminists,* who helped to mobilize the local and state organizations of the labor movement against the Gompers philosophy. The two outstanding social-feminist groups that played this great role were the National Consumers League under Florence Kelley and the Women's Trade Union League.

Both were substantially influenced by the fact that Europe and other civilized parts of the world were 'way ahead of the United States in this regard, and incidentally showed that none of Gompers' phantasmagorical predictions about the dire effects of social legislation on Freedom were coming true. (Readers of Sylvia Hewlett's *A Lesser Life* may be struck by the fact that she, too, was appreciably impressed by the difference between the U.S. and Europe, to the discredit of the country that she had liked to think was "advanced.") Kelley had joined the socialist movement in Europe; the W.T.U.L. had more than a leavening of socialist women inside it; Gompers' pontifications about Freedom did not confuse the social-feminists, by and large. The role of the National Consumers League may be misapprehended nowadays by confusion with organizations like Consumers Union, dedicated to product testing and evaluation; but Kelley's organization had nothing to do with this. It had been organized, and it functioned, as an auxiliary troop to aid the self-organization of workingwomen; it existed because the labor movement repudiated the organizing function it should have had in this regard. The National Consumers League sought to organize consumers' action (like boycotts) where women workers' organization was at stake.

It was the National Consumers League in 1910 that had initiated agitation in this country for minimum-wage legislation, while Gompers was denouncing "governmental paternalism" that would discourage union organization of women workers.[3]

This Gompers viewpoint was echoed by the E.R.A.-feminists once they had hardened their line on protective legislation. Their hearts bled for women workers, of course, just like Gompers' did, but women workers should go and organize themselves in trade unions, like the men, and *thus* better their conditions, instead of getting embarrassing laws put on the books... The social-feminists, of course, were *really* for women's trade-unionism, and thus knew only too well how difficult was that road to better conditions. They had a simple question to put: men workers had always had *two* weapons with which to fight, depending on the situation — self-organization (trade unions) *and* protective legislation. *Why should women workers be limited to one only (the first)?*

A prominent social-feminist, Alice Hamilton, explained in a published debate on the E.R.A., in 1924:

> ... it is not really accurate to call this an amendment for "equal rights" for both sexes, when practically it forbids one sex [women] to proceed along lines already tried and approved [labor legislation] unless the other sex will come too. Organized working men in the United States long since adopted the policy of seeking improvement in hours, wages, and conditions of work through their unions and not by legislation. [The last phrase is untrue.—H.D./S.D.] Women, whose labor organizations are young and feeble, have sought to secure reforms through legislation. This amendment would make it impossible for them to do so.[4]

This was unanswerable, and in fact never answered. Why was it fair, in the name of a pseudo-equality, to restrict women workers to the single weapon of trade-unionism? Just because men trade-unionists had adopted a certain policy (the Gompers policy)? Some of the Pure feminists' argumentation had a ring of plausibility only insofar as their audience swallowed A.F.L. ideology whole — a sad commentary on their feminism.

We need not doubt that the National Woman's Party could trot out a female trade-unionist who would testify that getting more money in her pay envelope made her feel "inferior" every Friday — just as the anti-E.R.A. sexist could produce many a woman who would testify that voting made *them* feel "unwomanly." In both cases the feeling is real. But the existence of these feelings is not an argument — it is the problem. *Only certain women, in certain situations, with certain backgrounds, feel threatened by special laws favoring women.*

The vice-chair of the National Woman's Party was quite frank on the subject of who these "certain women" are. In a 1924 debate with Mary Anderson, Gail Loughlin wrote the following. (The bracketed interpolations are added by us.)

> The restrictions placed upon the labor of women, unless removed, will shut the door of opportunity to women. [*What women is she talking about? Watch!*] Executive positions in the business or industrial world, which mean influences and high salaries, are never filled from the ranks of clock watchers. But a law diminishing the hours of labor for women makes all women clock watchers...
>
> Because such restrictions mean the closing of opportunity to women whose ability would enable them to rise to executive positions, the business and professional women of the country are nearly a unit in opposing them. ... The Woman's Party will never rest from its labors until Women [*the capitalized kind*] have reached the goal visioned by the great leaders of 1848 — the complete emancipation of women.[5]

In another magazine confrontation, the veteran advocate of Pure feminism Harriet Stanton Blatch took off after "welfare workers" who were "wrapping women in cotton-wool," in the course of a venomous attack on a Women's Bureau conference held in behalf of workingwomen. She denounced Florence Kelley for opposing the "home work" system — which was one of the most vicious forms of labor exploitation ever developed, especially to squeeze profit out of homebound women's labor. She triumphantly quoted a British report that expectant mothers "do not seem to suffer harm from working in factories." Of course she attacked the very idea of minimum-wage legislation.

Writing about the same Women's Bureau conference, Clara M. Beyer reported that the National Woman's Party had refused to send delegates unless granted special privileges; but —

> Whether the Woman's Party was officially represented or not, its point of view on industrial legislation was expressed by two of the speakers: Miss Merica Hoagland, of the Diamond Chain and Manufacturing Company of Indianapolis, and Mr. Charles Cheney, of Cheney Brothers, silk manufacturers of Connecticut. These speakers opposed industrial legislation for women as an interference with their property rights and their freedom of contract and an unnecessary discrimination against them in the labor market.[6]

We can think back to such eminently free contractual parties as the women workers on California's crops who asked for toilets in the fields, and wonder *whose* "property rights" Miss Hoagland and Mr. Cheney were worried about...

The current doctrine of the courts had a similar content. The minimum-wage law in the District of Columbia had just been quashed. The judges were not Fabians like Mrs. Blatch, but allegedly they were worried only about the interests of the proletariat: "no greater calamity," said the decision, "could befall the wage-earners of this country than to have the legislative power to fix wages upheld..."[7] This fused the N.W.P. philosophy with the Gompers doctrine.

All this — the drive against labor laws for workingwomen, in which the Pure feminists and the pure sweatshoppers worked hand in hand — was the predecessor of what was later known as the "Right to Work" movement, organized by industry's publicists after another world war. In both cases, in all such cases, proponents could show a number of injustices done to individual workers by prolabor laws that benefitted the vast majority (the Gladys Smith syndrome).

The National Woman's Party's E.R.A. campaign was, in effect, the first "Right to Work" movement.

From the beginning, the "Right to Work" ideology, with all of its fair-seeming appeal, continually peeped out of the agitation against special laws for workingwomen. Consider what happened in one 1919 confrontation at a New York State legislative hearing, where bills to improve workingwomen's conditions drew a mass supporting delegation rallied to Albany by the leading women's organizations. The opposition to these bills was also voiced by women, including two from the Equal Opportunity League which we have mentioned earlier, plus "Amy Wrenn, a Brooklyn lawyer, [and] Nora Stanton Blatch, an engineer of New York." (This Blatch was the daughter of the other.) The president of the Equal Opportunity League demanded "industrial equality." It was defined as "the right to work when and where she pleased."[8]

All labor laws to better working conditions interfere with this "right to work when and where etc." This was the central device of the Right to Work drive of the post–1945 period, and it was already in full flower as a device of the united front of the Pure feminists and impure industrialists that gathered strength in the '20s. Its proponents addressed themselves to certain women, as we see in Lemons' summary:

> From a position of early neutrality on the issue of protective legislation, business and professional women moved increasingly to oppose such laws. Class considerations entered because these women came to identify with management's view of industrial and labor questions. They saw industrial women as workers, not women.

This was a concise statement also of the mentality of the "business and professional women." Lemons continues:

> Moreover, they believed that the modest progress being made by business and professional women was being hindered by the protective laws. They came to feel in the late 1920s that their gains and position had not matched earlier expectations, and many felt threatened by legislation which sought to prevent the exploitation of industrial women.[9]

The basis for this turn was not simply that labor legislation which benefitted *other* women made these women feel "inferior." For one thing, there was an overlapping area between workingwomen in industry and "businesswomen"; for instance, there was the gray area between the cruelly exploited store clerks and the upwardly mobile women supervisors, assistant

77

managers, buyers, and so on. Some protective laws were so loosely formulated that their impact went needlessly beyond the work force itself; and at least part of the difficulty could have been eliminated by careful redrafting. But the would-be and could-be businesswomen were not interested in hearing about such an accommodation.

In the battleground of New York State, the lineup over labor legislation was a lesson in sociology. In one corner, the Women's Trade Union League mobilized allies like the Consumers League and the League of Women Voters. In the other corner, the Equal Opportunity League mobilized organizations of women journalists, doctors, dentists, lawyers, real-estate agents, and the activists of the women's clubs movement.

Yet it took several years before even the national organization of the business and professional women, the B.P.W.,* was weaned away from its social concerns and converted to Pure feminism — the kind that "saw industrial women as workers, not women," not *their* sisters. One reason, it seems, was happenstantial. During much of the 1920s the B.P.W.'s legislative chair was a socially conscious woman named Mary Stewart, who waged a battle against the N.W.P. elements in the organization and kept it neutral on the issue of labor laws — for a while. It was only in the late '20s that the N.W.P. viewpoint tended to become dominant, and, even so, it was not until 1937 that the B.P.W. endorsed the Pure amend-

---

* The National Federation of Business and Professional Women's Clubs (for short, B.P.W.) had been launched in 1918 as an offshoot of a War Department project to mobilize women for the wartime economy. With $65,000 allotted from military funds, a gathering of selected "women leaders" set up a small National Business Women's Committee, which then proceeded to call a convention in 1919 and set up the Federation. With the early slogan of "A Better Business Woman for a Better Business World," it stressed its stand for "genuine Americanism," against socialized medicine, and so on.[9]

ment. So difficult was it for the old concerns of social-feminism to be cast aside for what was easily seen as group selfishness.

Many state divisions of the B.P.W. had gone beyond their national organization in this direction. The N.W.P. had pioneered the road for these. For instance, the Indiana federation of the B.P.W. was involved in an outstanding job of alliance with the Manufacturers Association and right-wing business groups to kill progressive labor legislation in the state. Its organ mingled editorials reprinted from the N.W.P. and from the manufacturers' press. In 1928 it mobilized a united front of business and "civic" groups to block a proposed survey of state industrial conditions by the Women's Bureau, out of the express fear that this was "but a forerunner of the labor department's attempt to obtain an eight-hour day for the Indiana women." (Blocking the survey meant that they could continue to claim uninhibitedly that hundreds of thousands of Gladys Smiths had lost their jobs because of labor legislation.) These Pure feminists were so successful in their state that Indiana remained one of only five states that had no hours law.

They had important successes elsewhere, too. Impelled by its N.W.P. members, the Women's Lawyers Association took on a crusade against labor legislation for women. In California a proposed eight-hour law was defeated. A national Business Women's Legislative Council was formed by 1928 to make sure that workingwomen had at least the same right to be sweated as any men; a member of the N.W.P. became its president, and it endorsed the Pure E.R.A. in 1931. The first *major* women's organization to support the amendment was the B.P.W.; and indeed, as the N.W.P. faded in activity and weight, it was the B.P.W. that became the main proponent of the Pure E.R.A.

Before we leave this period, let us say a summary word about it *in relation to* the contemporary world better known to the reader, namely, the present time. It is a question of a couple of contrasts between then and now.

For one thing, the present-day reader may be a little surprised by the openness and uninhibited frankness of the alliance made between the union-busters of the National Association of Manufacturers (and similars) and the National Woman's Party. But in fact the liberal rhetoric had not yet become the all-compassing Newspeak of the establishment. We merely point this out without digressing further into sociopsychology. What forms the same alliance took after the Second World War are still to be seen.

For another and more important thing, we must record with some emphasis that the social-feminism of the 1920s, which we have been seeing in action, did not remain in existence in the postwar world. This is only part of a broader phenomenon which is not our subject. The Second World War and the postwar stagnation of radicalism produced a hiatus — a well-recognized break in continuity in the tradition and organization of leftist currents in the United States. The long tradition of social-feminism, a feminism furthermore allied with militant women trade-unionists, faded out in this same hiatus. When a "New Feminism" blossomed in the late 1960s, it emerged from a milieu that was unfortunately quite alien to the concerns of wage-earners, namely, from some circles of the predominantly middle-class student New Left at a time when this tendency was already crumbling into elitist and authoritarian fragments.

In consequence, as you read these words some decades later, there is no significant current that corresponds to the social-feminists of the 1920s and 1930s. An attempt was made especially in California, under the impulsion of Anne Draper, with the organization of Union W.A.G.E. (to be discussed later). But the present women's movement, as it exists in the public eye and as crystallized in groups like N.O.W., is the spiritual descendant of the National Woman's Party.

This movement, to be sure, contains at least a couple of shadings: there is the economic career-woman emphasis of the B.P.W. types, and there is the general-abstractionized feminism of the Alice Paul type. *Ms* magazine may lean toward the former and N.O.W. toward the latter, but the spread between is only from A to B.

This pattern is not gainsaid by the existence of a minor current that calls itself "Radical Feminism," articulated by Shulamith Firestone, for example. But in fact this current goes back explicitly to the ambiguous legacy of Alice Paul. Firestone insists on this connection, quite accurately. She reads most of previous feminism out of her tradition: "the majority of organized women in the period between 1890–1920 — a period usually cited as a high point of feminist activity — has nothing to do with feminism." This means *her* neofeminism has "nothing to do with" the social-feminism of the great days. What then is the feminism that Firestone recognizes? She bluntly traces the lineage of her "Radical Feminism" to "the militant Congressional Union subsequently known as the Woman's Party," and pays special homage to Harriet Stanton Blatch.[10]

Thus, social-feminism in the historical sense has been leached out of American society (though, as Sylvia Hewlett found on looking around, not in Europe), just as any and every liberal political tendency has given up any organizational existence in this country. And all that remains is the Pure feminism that made the Pure E.R.A. its banner, and that has yet to have a glimmering of comprehension of why the country refused to ratify it. Most if not all of the "New Feminist" activists have never even heard of the long historical connection between an equal rights amendment and the problems of workingwomen.

Most of them are not even aware of what happened to the E.R.A. as recently as the postwar period. We now turn to this chapter of the story.

7 The Stakes and the Players

By the 1930s, both the National Woman's Party and its Equal Rights Amendment were out of steam; both were slowly fading away. The N.W.P.'s ally, the National Association of Manufacturers, was little help during this decade. In the 1920s business spokesmen had euphorically claimed to represent eternal principles and eternal prosperity; but, as is well known, the 1930s made this talk unpopular. The spotlight was focused on economic problems. Of the activists we have seen in previous chapters, mainly the organized businesswomen of the B.P.W. were still much concerned with the E.R.A.

The Second World War gave feminism a new lift, just as the First had done. Once again the full integration of women into the system became especially attractive, as war emphasized the need of a society in crisis for complete mobilization of human resources.

The lead came from the Republican Party, which was going to retain its vanguard role in this area right up to the late 1960s. Behind this was the formation of an alliance of sorts — of the same informal sort as we have already seen in connection with the National Association of Manufacturers in the 1920s. In 1940, for the first time a major party platform endorsed the idea of an equal rights amendment. It was the Republican Party. The Democrats had to follow suit four years later, in time for the next presidential election.

However, neither party ever specifically endorsed the Pure E.R.A. as proposed by the N.W.P. and the B.P.W. This claim later became routine with E.R.A. propagandists, until "everybody" knew it was so and repeated it *ad lib;* but it is a myth. The platform planks carefully approved *an* amendment for equal rights for women, its content not further specified. Neither the N.W.P. nor the B.P.W. could get more specific language into the party platforms precisely in order to leave the door open for attempts to reconcile some sort of E.R.A. with women's labor legislation as well as with certain traditionalist notions about women's role. When the B.P.W. tried to get the parties to endorse "a constitutional amendment providing *unqualified* equal rights," both the Republicans and the Democrats deleted the crucial word.[1]

Still, it is probably true that the top leadership of the American political establishment was quite persuaded of the virtues of a Pure E.R.A., even if they had to draw back in practical politics. This opinion was held most firmly for over two decades by the main leadership of the Republican Party, for reasons that are quite clear.

Then, as later, the opposition to a Pure E.R.A., or to any E.R.A. at all, came from two disparate sources: (1) the pressure of the trade-union movement (now in favor of protective labor legislation and therefore opposed to the Pure E.R.A.) and of prolabor elements of various kinds, exercised through their links with the lib–lab left of the party structure, therefore strongest in sectors of the Democratic Party; and (2) the pressure of traditionalist notions on women's role in society as wife, mother, helpmeet, household slavery, etc., notions that were still dominant in a scattered fashion through most of the country.

In practice, these two motivations, while quite different in their roots, were intertwined for political effect, as often happens in Congress — intertwined sometimes out of ordinary dem-agogy, sometimes out of the ordinary American propensity for blurring social ideas. A spokesman for one motivation often mentioned the other also, to bolster the case. Two bisymmetric examples may be cited. (1) In a nationally televised debate a woman union official of the AFL-CIO, after incisively demonstrating what the Pure E.R.A. would do to workingwomen, added a traditionalist appeal about women's role.[2] (2) Senator Sam Ervin, who believed that both blacks and females were all right in their place, was always quite willing to mention the labor appeal after orating about his fears for the American home. Each type of speaker might use the other's appeals in passing.

A consequence is that, if we consider the political patterns in Congress on this subject for the whole period between the end of the war and the beginning of the 1970s, the first impression is that the issue cuts across all liberal–conservative lines as well as across party lines. Certainly the liberal wing of Congress, such as it was, was fragmented by a three-way split, as we will see. But the situation in the Republican Party was simpler.

The traditionalist type of opposition to the E.R.A. was naturally significant from the small-town and rural areas and their parochial politicians; and a couple of Republican senators from heavily industrial areas like New York State were affected by labor's position; but the bloc that was most easily emancipated from both of these pressures was the central bloc of Eastern-establishment Republicans, which was also the hub of the party leadership. And so, out of the crisscrossing of interests, ideas and power pressures, which made the issue a very thorny one on all sides, the most coherent lead came from the "purest" representatives of the power elite, untainted by either laborism or parochial traditionalism.

Only a few months after the end of the war, in July 1946, the issue was debated in the full Senate for the first time since the amendment had been introduced in its current form in 1923. The liberal–labor case against it was most cogently presented by Senator Robert F. Wagner of New York, who was also moved to include an unusual comment on the social lineup in the controversy:

> It is significant that testimony of sponsors of the pending proposal before the Senate committee shows the merest fragment of support from any person with industrial experience.

> The supporting organizations ... are made up of professional, cultural and patriotic types, many of them with very limited membership — all far removed from the problems of the majority of wage-earning women...

The opponents introduced no qualifying amendment; the vote took place only for-or-against the Pure businesswomen's version of equal rights. The result was that the amendment was defeated through failure to get the required two-thirds. But a majority of the senators voted in favor, 38 to 35.

The large majority of yeas were Republicans; the overwhelming majority of the nays were Democrats (plus the Progressive, La Follette).

The central issue was fairly clear in the course of the debate. As one senator put it: should the rights of women be equalized down or up? It was not an abstract issue, though arguments tended to be formulated abstractly. Radcliffe of Maryland, the senator in charge of floor-managing the E.R.A. resolution, at one point responded incautiously to the charge that its open-ended language would destroy a host of state laws favoring women: "women," he stated grandly, "are justly entitled to equality but no more." The practical meaning for workingwomen was that their conditions would be *equalized down,* while some career women might be gainers in upward equalization in upper-echelon job opportunities.

There was an easy and commonsense solution to one part of the problem, a solution supported by virtually every women's organization with the least pretense to liberalism. It was a test of the meaning of the political lineup over the E.R.A. The test was simply this: to pass a law with teeth providing for *Equal Pay for Equal Work* — pass it now, not merely promise action in some future year when a constitutional amendment might one day be ratified by the states.

The same session of Congress that acted on the E.R.A. was presented with an Equal Pay bill, a declaration of equal rights for women in the economic sphere. It had the advantage of *not* dividing women along stratified lines, for the B.P.W. favored this measure too. If the senators believed a fraction of the declamations in favor of Justice and Equality for women that were made on the floor in behalf of the E.R.A., the Equal Pay bill would have passed with near-unanimity. It needed only a simple majority, unlike the E.R.A. resolution which needed two-thirds. It would not need to be ratified by the states.

Yet the Equal Pay bill could not get to first base, in a Senate which voted by majority for the E.R.A.

"Look here, upon this picture, and on this..." Throughout the story of the E.R.A., the reader should ask the following question. If two-thirds of both houses, and eventually three-quarters of the state legislatures, could be hopefully won over for the Pure E.R.A. — which presumably abolished every conceivable species of obnoxious discrimination against women, and did so wholesale — why could not a mere majority of Congress (without the added hurdle of the state legislatures) be won to remedy only a few of the most crying injustices still being practiced?

In the same context: why couldn't an Equal Pay law, or even more sweeping abolition of sex discrimination, be adopted for the District of Columbia, by this same Congress?

Even a congresswoman, Sullivan of Missouri, rose in the House one day, October 12, 1971, to make this point a little bitterly about her pro-E.R.A. male colleagues. "It is easier," she said, "to convince the overwhelmingly male Congress and legislatures to strike a gallant blow for women by professing to be for equal rights than it is to sell those same men on the merits of treating women fairly in substantive legislation."

This suggests that there was something about the Pure amendment that made it quite acceptable to the same politicians who did not even pretend to be for Equal Pay. It suggests that there must have been a massive block of political motivation and social interest hidden beneath the Pure E.R.A.'s one-sentence blast. The fact that the E.R.A. could get a majority in the Senate (even if not two-thirds) raises this question sharply.

A few years later, the Washington political patterns were pushed even farther to the right with the fading of postwar illusions and the beginning of Cold War tensions and McCarthyite witchhunts. But for a while the E.R.A. did not falter and even forged ahead. As we will see, its main support still came from the established leadership of the Republican Party. Speeches in the Senate still orated about equal rights and Justice, while a bill for Equal Pay could not get past the same orators. Clearly this leadership of American politics expected something from the E.R.A. that was not immediately visible in its one-sentence blast about equal rights.

There was no mystery about what this latent meaning was to (say) the National Association of Manufacturers. If we move our attention from oratory over great principles to the practical question of dollars-and-cents, then we can learn the answer from the research economist Grace Hutchins. Using 1950 census reports and U.S. government agency figures, Hutchins calculated that, by paying lower wages to women than to men for similar work, the manufacturing companies realized *an additional profit of $5.4 billion* for the year. The extra profits thus gained from underpaying women formed 23 percent of all manufacturing company profits.[3]

These figures give some idea of the stakes, even if Hutchins' calculations are rough-edged. At stake is almost a quarter of all manufacturing profits in a gigantic economic structure. Governments have been overthrown for five percent.

The size of this stake bears on two aspects of the story that have been discussed. It makes clear why a bill to (in effect) expropriate a quarter of manufacturing profits, through *real* Equal Pay for Equal Work, had no chance of passage. And it makes clear that the Republican Party leadership was substantially convinced that the Pure E.R.A. would *not* enforce equal economic rights for the mass of women workers, whatever advantages it might mean for a minority. It *might* get more women on juries, and ameliorate other antiquated and secondary discriminations, but it would not equalize-up where it counted, in the countinghouses.

In the first period of the E.R.A.'s career, in the 1920s, these billions had been the stake of the second party in the open alliance of the National Woman's Party with the National Association of Manufacturers. The postwar world was different insofar as such a candid and public alliance was out of fashion. The new form of the N.W.P.–N.A.M. axis was now the *de facto* lineup of the B.P.W. organizations with the Republican Party leadership.

One other dollar figure would be useful to give this alliance its full refulgence. If manufacturing capital would lose something like several billions in profits given the enforcement of Equal Pay, how much would it gain, contrariwise, *if the whole network of women's labor legislation were destroyed throughout the states?* In realistic terms, what was the cash value of the Pure E.R.A. in dollars and cents to the hardheaded enterprisers who backed it on the unphilosophical side?

In the absence of authoritative statistics, we have only a broad hint at the immensity of the stakes. A Labor Department report on one year, 1969, noted that in a single state, California *violations* of the overtime and minimum-wage provisions netted employers more than $6 million. Since this is the gain due to *violations* of the law, multiply this figure by several score to get the sum that would be gained if these laws were entirely removed. Again, multiply by several times to take account of the dozens of other items of labor legislation that would be destroyed by the Pure E.R.A. Finally, since the figure cited was for California only, multiply by another number in order to extrapolate for the other forty-nine states.

Obviously, whatever the exact figure, the stakes run at least into the hundreds of millions of dollars, and in all likelihood mount into the billions — for one year.

It may be urged that this profit windfall from the Pure E.R.A. would be partially offset by the amendment's stimulation of the Equal Pay pattern. But there is an economic law that applies here in full force. When labor legislation is judicially destroyed, employers' immediate actions enforce the results very quickly, if not instantly; for pay and work rules are in their hands. But if and when an E.R.A. is said to call for raised wages, it will be many a moon before the difference becomes visible in the pay envelope. At the time this is being written, Title VII has presumably erased sex discrimination, but the differential between women's and men's pay (the former being 64 percent of the latter) has not changed substantially. Anyway, it does not take an E.R.A. to explain the pressure for an Equal Pay law, for this pressure was bound to mount quite independently of the E.R.A. agitation. In fact, E.R.A. activity has functioned in part as a safety-valve *lowering* the pressure for an Equal Pay law.

In any case, the stakes were high enough to convince a broad assemblage of establishment leaders in the country, above all Republican wheels. Here are some examples.

Richard Nixon boasted of being an endorser of the Pure E.R.A. from at least 1950 on — when virtually every liberal Democrat in politics condemned it. In March 1950 Nixon wrote to an N.W.P. member in his district that he would give his "full support to enactment of the bill," which was then being pushed in the House by Representative Katherine St. George. This early support won him high praise from the N.W.P., and gained their support of his Senate campaign against Helen Gahagan Douglas, whom the Paulite party called "equality's mortal enemy" (i.e., an enemy of the Pure amendment). Gerald Ford, whom Nixon later installed in the White House, was also an early supporter of the amendment, responding at the same time as Nixon to the N.W.P.'s inquiry with support for Katherine St. George's operation: "From the facts at hand I believe your views and mine coincide on this Amendment..."[4]

The Republican elder statesman, ex-president Herbert Hoover, endorsed the Pure amendment repeatedly beginning with the 1944 convention of the party. Eisenhower was the first president to include the amendment in his presidential program. Nixon's vice-president Spiro Agnew was a strong backer, as was

Nelson Rockefeller. In the Senate, the E.R.A. campaign of 1950–1953 was going to be managed by that patriarchal figure of right-wing Republicanism in California, Senator William F. Knowland. Among the most vocal proponents of the amendment have been a number of Senate figures whose names were, for a whole era, synonyms for the respectable right wing of American politics: Eastland, Stennis, Mundt, Thurmond, McCarran, et al. On the Democratic side, Presidents Lyndon Johnson and Kennedy have to be counted too. In 1968 George C. Wallace turned his attention away from combating civil rights for blacks and do-gooders, long enough to state: "If I am elected president of the U.S., I will do all in my power" for the Pure amendment. He ended this pledge with a tribute to — Mrs. O. H. P. Belmont, the rich socialite who had been one of the founders of the N.W.P.

One must ask whether these politician-pioneers of the Pure E.R.A., along with the National Association of Manufacturers, were converted to the noble objectives of human equality and justice by the sweet power of feminist arguments, or whether they knew indeed what they were doing.

8 The E.R.A. Murder Case

By 1950 Congress was ready to adopt *an* equal rights amendment, as advocated by the platforms of both major parties. An E.R.A. was, in fact, passed by the upper house by overwhelming votes — not once but twice, in 1950 and 1953.

Both of these measures looking to an equal rights amendment were killed — by the proponents of the Pure E.R.A. Let us hasten to add: this statement is not an exposé; the fact is uncontested, merely repressed and explained away.

Consider the following statement of fact: *We could have had a useful equal rights amendment on the books over a quarter century ago,* with a minimum of destructive effect on workingwomen and a maximum of benefit for all women; and by our time its implementation, however thorny, would have meant the elimination of a host of discriminatory laws and practices that still plague the status of women in our society.

The equal rights amendment that could have been adopted in 1950–1953, with a provision protecting workingwomen, was killed by a deliberate decision; and there is no question about who made that decision. It was made by the sponsors of the Pure E.R.A. — the sponsors in Congress, i.e., the central Republican leadership, captained by Senator Knowland, in concert with the sponsors outside, the businesswomen of the B.P.W. federation and the career-woman types of the National Woman's Party. The decision to kill came because the Senate had added an amending provision that would have the effect of making concessions to the interests of laboring women.

While the events themselves will show this clearly enough, it is a good thing that it was explicitly stated on the floor of the Senate — twenty years later — by the then spokesman of the Pure E.R.A. forces. On January 28, 1971, the Pure amendment's floor manager, Senator Birch Bayh, rose in the chamber to give an introductive speech in which he summarized the past history of the resolution.

(In Congress the proposal for a constitutional amendment takes the form of a Joint Resolution, which then refers the issue to the states.)

Wishing to show that the amendment had already been extensively debated, Senator Bayh recalled that it had been passed by the Senate in 1950 and 1953 with an offending addition, which the Pure called the "Hayden rider," i.e., an amendment proposed by Senator Hayden and adopted by the Senate. He related:

> All supporters of the [Pure] amendment agreed that the rider effectively destroyed the intended result of the amendment.... For this reason in the 86th Congress, after the Hayden rider had again been added during the floor debate, sponsors of the bill agreed to recommit it to the committee, *rather than have it enacted in that form.* [Italics added.]

It is clear that, rather than put the E.R.A. through *with* the Hayden addition, the Pure forces preferred to kill any E.R.A. Bayh went on to make clear that the sponsors had done exactly the same thing in the year before this speech (1970), and he summed up:

> However, when the operative language of the amendment was altered [in 1970] — by the very narrow vote of 36 to 33 — I agreed not to press for further floor action, in accordance with the advice of the women's groups who supported this measure. *Once again the amendment had been*

*killed as a result of changes in language adopted
on the floor.* [Italics added.]

The use of the passive voice ("the amendment had been
killed") avoided mentioning at this point just who had done the
killing. The speaker was naturally aware of the myth that had
been assiduously repeated for decades: the myth that it was the
prolabor supporters of the Hayden modification who were out to
kill any E.R.A. A frank statement of the facts behind the myth
would have gone like this:

> We, the proponents of the Pure E.R.A., are dis-
> mayed by your addition which adds a proviso
> protecting workingwomen (and therefore we have
> systematically adopted the dishonest claim that
> this addition is a "rider," that is, an unrelated
> amendment grafted onto a bill purely as a
> legislative trick).
>
> So you have killed *our* Pure E.R.A. for this
> session, and we shall therefore kill the E.R.A. that
> the Senate has adopted, by making sure it is
> buried in the House.

The principle is rule or ruin: better no equal rights
amendment at all than one that protects the special labor
legislation benefitting workingwomen.

Thus it was demonstrated that the two parties' platform
plank for "an equal rights amendment" had never been accepted
by the Pure faction, but rather secretly regarded as a danger to be
destroyed. It was also shown that the sponsors were for the Pure

E.R.A. not *in spite of* its possible effects on workingwomen but only because of this aspect. There were a number of would-be E.R.A. compromisers, seeking an agreement between the camps, until they learned it the hard way. We will see compromise efforts, one of the last being made by Birch Bayh himself; and their fate will be instructive.

In the early 1950s the pro-E.R.A. sentiment in Washington seemed overwhelming. A woman lawyer wrote in the American Bar Association's *Journal* that "it is considered fashionable on Capitol Hill to be for the amendment."[1] It was backed not only by the party platforms but actively by the Women's Divisions of both major parties. The top Republican leadership came out for the Pure E.R.A., as did the most conservative women members of both houses. In the Senate, Senator Margaret Chase Smith of Maine saw "protective legislation" for women as a personal insult, for (she explained) women were really stronger than men.

In 1950 the E.R.A. was floor-managed in the House by Representative Katharine St. George, the very model of the N.W.P. type of feminist since the days of Mrs. Belmont. As *Colliers* magazine admiringly described her at the time, she was an "arch-Republican from Tuxedo Park, New York, the ultrasmart stone-walled community created by the rich in the state's 29th Congressional District. ... Her background is strictly social-register, Junior League, grand balls in the gay capitals of Europe."[2] She had married into the First National Bank of New York, but eventually became interested in social affairs of a different sort. In Congress since 1946, this ornament of Republican conservatism was accustomed to attacking the Truman administration for "trying to socialize the U.S." Needless to say, she insisted that "women neither need nor want protective legislation. They want to be free to work as equals, asking for no special privileges..."[3] Who else was in such little need of more special privileges?

As if to complement the picture for future researchers in historical parables, there was another woman in the House in 1950: Helen Gahagan Douglas of California, a good Democratic liberal; later that same year she was going to be witchhunted out of an election victory by that firm supporter of the Pure E.R.A., Richard Nixon. Douglas announced on the floor, even though the matter had not yet come up in the lower chamber, that she would support only an E.R.A. modified by the Hayden amendment. The best-known proponent of this position was Mrs. Eleanor Roosevelt.

In the Senate, the Pure E.R.A. forces gave management of the resolution to a conservative Democrat, Gillette of Iowa. The Senate Judiciary Committee, a citadel of sobersided traditionalism, had reported it out favorably, as it always did before and after. Its vote was unanimous. Gillette introduced it into the Senate on January 19, 1950, with the sponsorship of 32 other senators.

The opposition to the Pure E.R.A. divided into two unequal camps. Senator Carl Hayden (Dem., Arizona) introduced his amendment to the resolution, to combine the liberal–labor objectors with some of the traditionalists. It provided that the new constitutional article "shall not be construed to impair any rights, benefits or exemptions now or hereafter conferred by law upon persons of the female sex."

Hayden's own argumentation strongly emphasized the views of the women's organizations, trade unions, American Civil Liberties Union, etc. who opposed a Pure E.R.A. He offer-ed his amendment, he said, as a means of taking the curse off the old proposal:

> I offer this amendment because there can be no
> question that it is the deliberate intention of those
> who sponsor this change in the Constitution
> completely to eradicate from the statute books
> every law in every state which confers any right,
> benefit, or exemption to women which is not also
> available to men.[4]

The Senate debate provided no surprises, but we must survey the various strategies.

The Pure E.R.A. proponents offered a series of set speeches glowing with elocution in praise of justice, sex equality, human rights, and the virtues of womankind. Against these abstract declamations, the liberal wing spoke much of the concrete problems of particular sectors of the so-much-acclaimed ranks of womankind as affected by the Pure one-sentence blast.

The traditionalist speakers went easy on their underlying fears about the American Home and Family, and were even closermouthed on that unmentionable, the need to maintain male supremacy. They were most cogent when they con-centrated on the juridical difficulties that the Pure E.R.A. would encounter. They demonstrated with considerable technical success that to try to excise sex prejudice and discrimination from the tangled body of American law and life by means of the Pure one-sentence was like trying to cut out a tumor with a meat cleaver. Whatever their own operative motivation, this limited argument meshed part-way with the socioeconomic demonstrations of the liberals, who were also showing that the meat cleaver could make deep gashes in the interests of workers.

As we saw earlier, the long-standing position of liberal and leftist women and of the labor movement was to oppose *any*

constitutional amendment as unwise. This position of flat opposition to the E.R.A. route was retained by a group of the most
liberal and prolabor senators, led by Herbert Lehman of New
York, Estes Kefauver of Tennessee, and Wayne Morse of
Oregon — three of the most consistent liberals who ever got
themselves elected to the Senate. But this group did not confine
itself to negation. Kefauver introduced a substitute proposal.

This substitute was effective in showing up the hypocrisy of
most of the E.R.A.-feminism that was swamping over the
Congress. It was a "Women's Status" bill drawn up along the
lines advocated by the National Conference on Labor Legislation held in Washington the previous December. It sought to
remove "any remaining discriminations against women in the
law" and elsewhere, and at the same time "to preserve provisions
of labor legislation which have proved beneficial to working
women" — to "establish a policy ... of non-discrimination on the
basis of sex ... while at the same time safeguarding legislation of
benefit to women..." The bill declared "that it is the policy of the
Federal Government to abolish distinctions based on sex in
Federal law and its administration, except such as are reasonably
justified by differences in physical structure or maternal
function," and would apply to state governments as well. It set
up machinery to implement the goals by specific steps.

Here was a bill setting out in concrete legislative terms what
equal rights could mean from the standpoint of the great majority
of the female population. Remember, again, that this bill needed
only a majority, not two-thirds, and did not need state
ratification.

This Women's Status bill was overwhelmingly defeated in
the vote, 65–18. Though at this point it was offered as a
substitute for the E.R.A., in later debates similar proposals were

offered as independent alternatives; no matter. The proponents of Pure Justice for Women gave it short shrift, even though their orations about the Rights of Womankind would have seemed to require immediate adoption by acclamation. The reader is again asked to wonder why only the Pure E.R.A. aroused the enthusiastic approbation of defenders of the established status quo.

Kefauver's presentation of the bill did stir one senator to make an immediate rebuttal that was of great interest. Kefauver had ended with a challenge to the Pure advocates with regard to the drafting of women in war.* Senator Harry Pulliam Cain of Washington state, then one of the most noted rightists in the capital, rose to make a point that dominated the *New York Times* account of the entire session.

"If and when there is a war in the future," he said, "we are going to need, more than we have ever previously obtained, the services of every man, woman, and child, in the world of tomorrow." The adoption of E.R.A., he argued, "would make available to our Government all the people of America without reference to sex." His motivating concern was the organization of total war for the grand conflict, and to this end he cited the Red enemy as the model: "in the last war the Russians appeared to me to have had a far better comprehension and under-standing of what total war really meant than all the other nations put together..."

---

* The Women's Status bill left this vexed question open for separate determination. Whatever one's views on women and the draft, why should the legal enforcement of (say) the Equal Pay principle have to depend on *first* convincing the populace that women should carry guns for the state? The Pure feminists often give their views an ultimatistic thrust — by insisting, for example, that every possible symbol of women's inferiority must be overthrown in one fell swoop — and this often appears to be very "radical." It is only a sectarian mind-set; it is the rhetorical side of the career woman's valuation of social-status symbols over lower-class working conditions. Leading proponents of the Pure E.R.A. often reduced their case to the "symbol" argument alone, as we will see below.

Cain let this argument out, but such considerations were usually as underground among the Pure E.R.A. supporters as the Male Supremacy issue was among the traditionalists. By the nature of the case, "you don't talk about such things, you do them." We have already remarked that both world wars gave feminism a decisive boost for similar considerations, leading to the acceptance of women's suffrage after the First World War, and to the turn to E.R.A. after the Second.

The Senate debate on the E.R.A. itself was as blurred as experienced politicians could manage.[5] Gillette of Iowa, the Senate floor manager, tried to obscure the issues by claiming that *all* senators should vote for the resolution just in order to submit the issue to the states. Senator Margaret Chase Smith likewise endorsed the idea of (others) voting *for* the Senate resolution but opposing the E.R.A. in the states. She testified that the Pure E.R.A. was going to get the votes of some senators "though they do not believe in equal rights."

Gillette's statements on the meaning of the Pure amendment were guaranteed to puzzle a Supreme Court that might some day try to determine what Congress had in mind. The amendment, he said,

> does not, as many suppose, deal with men or women. It deals with governments and the law made by governments.... It grants no new, as yet unheard-of rights.... This is most certainly a rigid limitation upon its applicability.

He made an attempt to confront Hayden's amendment to the resolution. He did not bring himself to admit that the Pure amendment would, or even might, destroy labor legislation for women. He preferred to think that labor laws would be applied to men too; but what if...? "The decision would be in the hands of each State." The Pure advocates had always denied this leeway, but Gillette's statements were so dim and dark that nothing he said meant much.

Senator Margaret Chase Smith, who was accustomed to speaking for all womankind, was more forthright: "I am in favor of the proposed equal rights amendment to the constitution for the very reason which causes some women to oppose it. ... [For] when women demand equal rights with men they must give up their special feminine privileges..." This was the straight, undiluted N.W.P. line.

The final outcome had much to do with the crisscrossing motivations and strategies — the uneasy alliance of the liberal-prolabor wing and the traditionalists, the confuse-the-cat strategy of the Republican managers of the debate, the split in the liberal wing itself, the tension between the doctrinaire rigidity of the N.W.P. line and the apprehensive flexibility of the Republicans, and so on. The Hayden amendment to the resolution won handily, no doubt because of its joint appeal to both the liberals and some traditionalists. The Haydenized E.R.A. was then adopted by a vote of 63 to 19, well beyond the required two-thirds. The party lineup was instructive: in the final tally, all Republicans answering voted yea; and of the 19 nays, all were Democrats, including Senator Lehman. We will come back to the question of various motivations behind the vote.

For the first time, an E.R.A. had been voted by a house of Congress. Out of the tangle of motivations had come a constitutional article that *could* be a landmark in the battle against legal sexism, even though the latter would not be abolished in one blow. What the Hayden E.R.A. *could* have meant was the historic establishment of a legal base line from which the continuing struggle for equality could proceed to strike blows against other bastions of sexism. (We will see that even the Pure E.R.A. could not do more than that in reality.)

All wings of the women's movement, together with labor and civil rights advocates in general, could have worked together for important objectives, no longer split along social lines. One of the consequences of the Hayden E.R.A., as of the Pure thing, would be this: every court and administrative body would have to work on the presumption that sex discrimination was guilty until proved innocent.

All this without impairment of workingwomen's conditions by destruction of labor legislation. And this was precisely why the Hayden E.R.A. had to be scuttled and killed — even though, as the *New York Times* reported, the great victory was publicly hailed by "jubilant" supporters of the E.R.A.

In view of the public "jubilation," the Hayden E.R.A. had to be killed in the dark — mugged. How this was done, and by whom, is now part of the public record. But at the time there was no account given in the press (that we have been able to find) explaining to the "jubilant" public why the great victory over sexism disappeared from the halls of Congress after the historic Senate vote. Three years later (we find) a line in the *Times* mentioned that it had "died in the House Judiciary Committee" in 1950.

At the time, Alice Paul, the N.W.P.'s leader, hinted to the press what was to happen: "It is impossible to imagine the Constitution containing two such paragraphs" — that is, containing both the Pure statement and the Hayden addition; and she indicated that her strategy would be to get it through the House of Representatives in its original Pure form. But this raised the fear that, once the issue was before the House, it might be the Senate version that would win out. Before long, the N.W.P. turned its activists' attention toward scuttling the whole thing for the nonce. *The new E.R.A. was buried in the House committee through the exertions of the N.W.P.*

This is the account given twenty-five years later by Alice Paul herself, in her Oral History memoirs.[6] The following points deserve mention first.

> ○ As Alice Paul remembers it, the Hayden E.R.A. would have gone through swimmingly if it had not been hatcheted in the corridors by an N.W.P. emergency mobilization of forces to avert this danger.

> ... you know [related Paul in her memoirs], they *nearly* got it through in 1950, almost got it through... Well, now, if it *had* gone through, it would have gone on to the states and probably been ratified, and here we would have had it in the Constitution, as a result of all these years of labor, inequality written in for women!

The "inequality" was constituted by the preservation of labor legislation for workingwomen. In 1950, among the things that Paul discovered to her horror was that the E.R.A. was *not* being stalled by the Congressional machinery; on the contrary, "a very active campaign was afoot to send it on to the states for ratification." Now the N.W.P. faction was discommoded by the scam which Senator Gillette had used in the Senate, namely, the pretense that one's position on the issue didn't matter, but everyone should vote to send it on for the states' decision.

The N.W.P.'s activist core, organized by Alice Paul herself, went into high gear to prevent this, by lining up the House leaders, especially the Republicans, to kill the resolution by asphyxiation. Paul's memoirs exude pride as she recalls how effective this wrecking crew was.

○ Alice Paul's memoirs do not slander Senator Hayden, unlike some accounts that owed their venom to imagination. Paul testifies that Senator Hayden was a strong supporter of equal rights, one of the best. Says she (in her memoirs): "a very fine man, Mr. Hayden. Very, very, *very* friendly to the cause of women. And he was known, and famous almost, for the things that he did" for women employees of the Senate. He "just couldn't possibly be ... more kindly and more concerned," she adds, and again attests to his "complete good will and good intentions."

○ It is not digressive to mention another horrible discovery that Alice Paul made at this time: the discovery that the Washington representative of the B.P.W. itself, Marjory Temple, was actually in favor of the Hayden E.R.A. and was actively working for it. National leaders of the B.P.W. were hastily called to Washington to scotch this snake-in-the-grass. At the end of the session, a new president of the B.P.W. proceeded to fire Temple. But we never find out from Alice Paul's recollections just how the B.P.W.'s most active worker for the E.R.A. could get enthusiastic about a measure which the Pure publicists' mill later painted as simply a conspiracy against women's rights.

The N.W.P.'s emergency mobilization in Washington to kill the Senate's E.R.A. is documented in some detail, nowadays, in the organization's microfilmed *Papers* presently deposited in libraries. The organization's attitude quickly went through a first stage — the aforementioned jubilation over the adoption of the E.R.A. resolution even if Haydenized. A letter from the group's Publicity Committee chair, addressed to leading party members, expressed this jubilation and belied the later line of invective against the same amendment:

> This afternoon [wrote Florence Armstrong] the Senate passed the ERA.... [T]hus a long step forward has been taken in our effort to raise the status of women.... [T]he victory in the Senate is a glorious advance regardless of the harmful Hayden amendment. The nation is hearing from every radio commentator this evening about the ERA. Every paper will carry it. Everyone will now take it seriously.[7]

But more influential leaders of the N.W.P. were not carried away by the jubilation. With the doctrinaire rigidity of which Alice Paul was herself the incarnation, they counterposed a contrary line: the Haydenized E.R.A. was *worse* than nothing. This sentiment was expressed in a letter from the N.W.P. Congressional Committee's co-chair, Emma Guffey Miller, addressed to the party chair: "I would rather have women remain as they are than suffer such an amendment [as Hayden's]."[8]

The main enemy was identified: the labor movement. Miller's letter stated that the Hayden addition "was backed by Secretary [of Labor] Tobin and Labor." Another party activist wrote Alice Paul that "It goes without saying that UNION LABOR IS OUR REAL ENEMY IN ALL THIS." (Capitals in original.)[9]

The N.W.P.'s and Tuxedo Park's woman in Congress, Representative Katherine St. George, promised to push the Pure E.R.A., but she was not encouraging: her "hopes of getting the [Pure] amendment passed grow dimmer every day."[10] As this alternative faded, the party leadership began discussion of a second course of action: writing a substitute for the Hayden amendment that would leave the Pure content unblemished. This would change the Hayden wording, following his "pattern but not his result." One version of this course proposed the following substitute:

> This article shall not be construed to impair any rights, benefits, exemptions, or protections conferred equally upon men and women, or any special consideration given to women on grounds of motherhood.[11]

Another version left out the "motherhood" exemption. Discussions of this possible course went on inside the N.W.P. for some months. At one point a number of Congressmen were approached with new wordings. But eventually the ultimatistic "all or nothing" approach won out.

N.W.P. activists were pressing the ultimatistic position on Alice Paul by March — for example:

> I believe it would be better to go all out against the [Hayden] rider. Any attempt to meet opponents of your Amendment in a conciliatory

spirit will be construed against you as an admission that, by the very nature of things, there must be a difference in laws applying to men and women. And this is wholly inconsistent with your position.

Another letter rejecting any "conciliatory spirit" argued that "we" would "lose our own self-respect" by com-promising.[12]

Besides, St. George, who was trying to get 218 signatures to pry the amendment out of the Judiciary Committee and put it on the floor, was becoming more and more fearful that this course was dangerous: if the issue reached the floor, the same "rider" that had ridden through the Senate so easily might be attached again. Wouldn't this risk the purity of the Pure amendment? As one party activist wrote to the party chair:

> ... we may be walking into a trap. If we get the 280 [*sic*] needed the amendment comes up for an immediate vote and could have the Hayden amendment put on and pass in twenty minutes.[13]

In March, Alice Paul herself decided to pull the rug from under the House discharge petition. "It seems to me dangerous for us to push the Petition any further," she wrote. Success would mean that "the control of the Amendment passes out of our hands." A House vote would be "premature," i.e., the Pure amendment might lose.[14]

The final course decided on, then, was to keep the amendment buried in the House Judiciary Committee, naturally looking forward to the day when Congressional opinions would be changed.[15] And this is what was carried out, with a minimum of public notice. In her memoirs Alice Paul later recalled: "Both sides, Republican and Democrat, we worked just on them. And we did get enough of them to agree not to bring it up, and it wasn't brought up. And that session came to an end."[16] At the December 1950 meeting of the N.W.P. National Council, Anita Pollitzer, who had worked out the line with Alice Paul, introduced a motion to suppress any action on the amendment in this Congress, and this motion was passed unanimously.[17]

The E.R.A. was now dead for the next period, killed by the Pure at heart.

After this successful murder, the Pure faction spread the tale that it was the "Hayden rider" that did the killing. By this they merely meant that the Hayden amendment had "forced" *them* to kill the E.R.A. off.

But the tangled motivations already referred to were more tangled than that. It may be surmised, though not documented, that wise Senate operators may well have figured in advance that the Republican-cum-N.W.P./B.P.W. alliance *would* kill an amended E.R.A. A different coil of the tangle involves, perhaps, Senator Kefauver, who voted with the majority for E.R.A. in the final ballot, whereas Senator Lehman voted nay (though three years later, incidentally, he followed Kefauver's course). For this wing of the liberal Democrats, the sponsors of the Women's Status bill, the Hayden E.R.A. was simply a lesser evil, acceptable because it averted the greater evil of the Pure amendment. On the other side, a somewhat analogous lesser-evil attitude probably characterized some of the traditionalists who wound up voting with the majority. And to this tangle, add the outright opponents of women's rights who voted for the Pure E.R.A. or any E.R.A. on the ground that Gillette had suggested, i.e., the slippery ground that Congress' vote on a constitutional amendment is only a decision to submit the issue to the states.

But all these tangled ratiocinations, machinations and maneuvers are the common small-change of Washington politics. As laws emerge (somehow) out of the raveled welter of political infighting and compromise, it is the more or less objective meaning of the laws that eventually dominates. What the Hayden E.R.A. would have meant for the women's rights movement would have been independent of whatever went on inside Hayden's skull or any other's. In American politics the best example of this truth came later, when in 1964 Title VII of the Civil Rights Act was amended to include sex along with race — mainly as a ploy *by the Southern racists* to get the act defeated. Title VII, which subsequently played much of the role that an E.R.A. would have done, and which became the most powerful weapon against legal sexism, owes its existence on the books to the foulest of political motives. (We will come back to this in the next chapter.)

The N.W.P. fable, endlessly repeated by the E.R.A.-feminists, runs up against some objective facts, even on the lowest level, i.e., personal motivations. One we have already seen: Alice Paul's emphatic endorsement of Senator Hayden's *bona fides.* Another is this: the list of senators who sponsored the Pure amendment, that is, the thirty-odd who joined Gillette of Iowa in presenting the resolution to the Senate, surely did not consist in their majority of duplicitous conspirators scheming to sully the Purity of the amendment with a "rider." But we must report that after the discussion, only about a half of *these* senators voted against the Hayden addition. Only half of the sponsors themselves!

Anyway, it was only Hayden who was able to get an E.R.A. through. This point was strongly made by Hayden himself when the whole scenario was replayed in 1953.

In the 1953 Congress, the Republican Party was even more openly in charge of the E.R.A. operation. The manager of the resolution was Senator John Marshall Butler of Maryland, a Republican; the sponsor list this time was overwhelmingly Republican; and the guiding spirit hovering over it was the GOP's Senate leader, William F. Knowland, who was regarded as a reactionary even by some conservatives. Knowland had been hailed at that year's National Woman's Party convention when it was announced that he would throw his influence behind their E.R.A. and get it through the upper house. With Knowland around, the N.W.P. did not have to flaunt its alliance with the National Association of Manufacturers.

Knowland was as good as his word, and on July 16, 1953 the Pure E.R.A. was taken up by the Senate, as Congresswoman Katherine St. George again stood by in the House awaiting its passage. Hayden continued the replay by reintroducing his amendment. On the Senate floor he emphatically made the challenging statement that the E.R.A. could be adopted *only* with his amendment. The swing vote in 1950, he argued, was cast by senators "who would not have voted for the original amendment, but who did vote for the equal rights proposal after it had been amended." There could be little doubt about the accuracy of this statement.

A question was thrown to Hayden from the floor: "Are we to understand the object of the amendment of the Senator from Arizona is to make clear that the laws passed for the benefit of women would not be denied them because of the equal rights amendment, if adopted?" Hayden replied with an emphatic yes, specifying the interest of "laboring women throughout the Nation" in their state laws.

The importance of this exchange, and others like it, has little to do with individuals' motives or psychiatric analyses. Rather, it forms part of the legislative record, which will later be examined by the courts to help fix the juridical meaning of the law as passed. (This is another reason why the Pure habit of ascribing sinister conspiratorial motives to the "Hayden rider" is not a serious analysis, however useful as a propaganda fable.)

On the other hand, the Pure amendment's floor manager, Senator Butler, provided a different sort of material for future judicial interpretations. *He* provided evidence that the aim of the Pure amendment was to wipe out such laws as "a minimum wage law for women." Here is the passage which might settle the question for a Supreme Court opinion:

> I had great hope that with the adoption of the Fourteenth and Nineteenth amendments the United States Supreme Court would follow up its earlier decision and remove the existing discrimination against women [he means *for* women's interests], but in *The West Coast Hotel Co.* case (300 U.S. 379), a minimum wage law for women was upheld, whereas a similar statute in the District of Columbia had been declared to be unconstitutional as contravening the right of contract. So ... there is a sharp division of opinion in the Supreme Court of the U.S. which points up the necessity of a constitutional amendment if the problem is to be adequately solved.[18]

This was a binding statement about just *why* an E.R.A. was a "necessity" that would not be heard in the welter of E.R.A. propaganda. According to the E.R.A.'s floor manager, the amendment was a necessity in order to "remove" laws like the minimum wage law.

At this 1953 session, the liberal Democrat faction introduced a Women's Status bill not as a substitute to the E.R.A. but as an independent measure. Unlike 1950, the sponsors of the Pure amendment had to figure out how on earth they could vote against it, after their own orations about women's rights; but vote against it they did. *This* bill had teeth.

At this session, Senator Lehman spoke strongly in favor of the Hayden E.R.A. He had an impact. Senator Langer of North Dakota, one of the resolution's sponsors, chairman of the Judiciary Committee that had reported it in, openly wavered on the floor. Langer, who had some reputation as a Republican maverick, said he was thinking of moving recommitment so that an amendment could be drafted to cover the objections made by Lehman, objections that reflected the most consistent liberal–labor position. Lehman assured him he would welcome this. But floor manager Butler jumped up to remonstrate, the whip hissed through the air, and immediately Langer withdrew his suggestions, in so many words giving as his reason Butler's intransigence.

The Republican command had scotched another effort to reconcile E.R.A. aims with labor interests. But their repression worked only on their own ranks. The outcome was a repetition of 1950. The Hayden addition was passed by 58 to 25. Once again, out of the Republican-weighted list of sponsoring senators only about a half voted against the Hayden formula. In the final vote on the E.R.A. as amended, the measure was carried by the much-increased majority of 73 to 11.

No matter; the E.R.A. was once again murdered anyway, buried in the House in the same way as before, by the decision of the Republican leadership in alliance with the B.P.W. businesswomen and the N.W.P.-type feminists.

9 Title VII Takes the Trick

The 1950–1953 push for the E.R.A. had emerged from the favorable postwar climate; it was a weak analogue of the feminist drive that had followed the First World War and which had ended with the suffrage victory. But by the time the 1953 session of Congress was over, the climate had chilled: the country was well into both the Cold War and the "McCarthyite" period, in which Senator Joe McCarthy witchhunted the Truman administration and the Truman administration witch-hunted "reds." The swing to conservatism in political style pushed the E.R.A. — which presented knotty problems to conservatives — into the background. (We will have another word to say on this climate at the beginning of the next chapter.)

In fact, the next time the E.R.A. reached the Senate floor, in July 1960, support for the Pure amendment was very weak. Senator Lyndon Johnson routinely introduced the resolution with no supporting argumentation and immediately turned the floor over to Senator Hayden, who proposed his amendment as before. In the course of doing so, he made two arguments. One we have already seen: without the Hayden amendment, no two-thirds majority could be gained to put the resolution through. The second argument was that this amendment was the only way to prevent the ambiguously worded Pure E.R.A. from being tied up in the courts for years to come — by "an infinite number of lawsuits and in endless litigation."[1]

> Before court interpretation could clarify the intent and meaning of the joint resolution [the E.R.A.], many years would elapse during which it is not only possible, but probable, that rights, benefits and privileges now enjoyed by women throughout the United States would be denied to them.

Thereupon the Hayden amendment was added to the resolution (that is, to the Pure form) by a mere voice vote! Taken aback, Senator Butler — the 1953 floor manager for the Pure E.R.A. — moved to send the resolution back to the Judiciary Committee, and this was done. Butler's words reflect the strangeness of this whole episode:

> It is a very strange procedure that a proposed constitu-tional amendment should be brought before the Senate apparently with no sponsor and nobody to manage the joint resolution. To say the least, I was shocked when the Amendment offered by the Senator from Arizona [Hayden] was accepted, on a voice vote, after very little debate, with no one to present the other side.

He, Butler, disclaimed the post of manager of the resolution, but asked the Senate to have the "courtesy" of conferring a "parent" on the thing. On the other side, Hayden certainly did not object to having the issue referred back to the committee, where (he said) his side would provide testimony in its favor at hearings to be held. No hearings were ever held. In this Strange Interlude, no one was very eager to get involved with the E.R.A. issue.

This is how the situation remained for the decade or so during which the political climate of the country went through a big change, the Great Hiatus of the American left, the period which marked the broken line of continuity — between the old alliance of liberals and left around social-feminism, on the one hand, and on the other the peculiar "New Left" that arose in the 1960s, especially the mid–'60s.*

Whatever the reasons, the E.R.A. remained frozen in place on the Congressional calendar for over a decade. When the issue of women's rights began to thaw out in the '60s, it first popped out of the legislative locker in unexpected fashion, indeed semiaccidentally. To wit: in the Civil Rights Act of 1964, which we have already mentioned.

This development was not the outcome of a push by a feminist movement; the "New Feminism" had not yet come into existence; Washington was still being cultivated by the Business and Professional Women's federation (B.P.W.), about which there was nothing new.

The Civil Rights Act was drawn up to ban discrimination on the basis of *race, color, religion, or national origin.* Under its Title VII, the section on employment, the word *sex* was inserted in addition. This proposal came not from liberals, nor from the politicians who made orations in favor of Womankind whenever the E.R.A. came up. It came from conservative Southerners *in a maneuver to get the bill killed.*

Here, for example, is the account by Robert Smuts in his *Women and Work in America:*

> When Judge Smith of the Rules Committee expanded the bill to prohibit discrimination based

---

* To complicate the picture, this New Left was later frequently accused by women participants of being sexist, antifeminist, and shot through with Male Supremacy prejudices at least in practice. To what extent these charges are justified, or, perhaps more to the point, to what New Leftish circles these charges most applied — this is a question of which the present authors cannot speak confidently. Although the accusatory women think this is an independent question, such features of certain New Left circles were closely connected with other ways in which these New Leftists abandoned the ideas and traditions of the preceding socialist movement, in the belief that they were improving on the "Old Left," which frequently included democratic Marxism. We can take note of, but not settle, this problem.

on sex, he believed that he was giving the *coup de grâce* to a bill designed to outlaw discrimination based on race. He could not believe that his colleagues would consider giving broad federal protection to women by prevent-ing their being discriminated against in the work arena. But Congress passed the Civil Rights Act with the provision on sex discrimination included.[2]

The Southerners had miscalculated; the pressure for civil rights was stronger than they believed. So the racists got an installment of women's rights into the law, *without* a provision to preserve women's protective legislation.*

The N.W.P. proceeded to use the new Title VII as their tool in their continuing battle against protective legislation for wom-en. For example, in early 1967 the same N.W.P. ex-chair whose probity we have footnoted, Ernestine B. Powell, in response to directives from Alice Paul, joined the National Association of Railroad Business women in a lawsuit against the state of Ohio in order to wipe out a state law limiting the working hours of women railroad employees. The Columbus *Dispatch* wrote it up as a sort of crusade:

A phone call came from headquarters. The order: turn Ohio into a battleground. The fight, as old as Adam and Eve, is equal rights for women. The hour of the battle will depend on what the Ohio

---

* Some enterprising Paulites made an attempt to claim credit for this political windfall. Asked about the inclusion of "sex" in Title VII, a former N.W.P. chair, Ernestine B. Powell, told the press: "It was a great achievement," not a fluke but "a long hard fight and we won."[3] Madison Avenue types look on this sort of thing as routine publicism, though on other avenues it is called prevarication. An examination of the N.W.P.'s Papers shows there was no intensive activity characteristic of the party when it sought to pull off a legislative coup. The common knowledge and report that the inclusion of "sex" in Title VII was the doing of the Southern racists is confirmed (for anyone who needs confirmation) by a legislative history and analysis written by R. J. Celada of the Library of Congress.[4]

legislature does with protective legislation for women during the present session. The call came to Columbus attorney Ernestine B. Powell from the Washington D.C. headquarters [of the N.W.P.] who was marshaling her forces for a skirmish in Ohio, using this state as a test case of Title VII of the Civil Rights Act of 1964.[5]

The N.W.P. drive to wipe out protective legislation had many successes, but Title VII was a more limited instrument than a Pure E.R.A. would have been; to take one example, it applied only to employers of 25 or more employees. The consequences of Title VII were also more mixed than a Pure E.R.A. would be, but we cannot here take the space that would be needed to sketch all the intricacies of this legal machinery. We are here concerned with a secondary effect, namely, the impact on the fight around the passage of a Pure E.R.A. *in addition* to Title VII.

The agency set up to implement Title VII was the Equal Employment Opportunity Commission (E.E.O.C.). It dealt mostly with racial discrimination in hiring, but, since the sex issue *had* been written in the commission began to enforce this provision too, after some hesitation. This led to a confrontation with the "protective laws" of the states much like the confrontation expected to result from a Pure E.R.A.

The E.E.O.C. tended to rule that, when there was a claim of conflict with women's labor legislation, Title VII superseded the states' laws. In 1969 it laid down as its guiding principle that the state laws are irrelevant and in conflict with Title VII. Thus, at least in part, the drive to destroy the whole body of labor legislation for women came in fact not from the passage of a

Pure E.R.A., as had been feared, but came from this unplanned quarter.

The element of chance and accident is not as important as may appear. For a half century and more, powerful interests had been probing this and that avenue of approach to *"get"* those labor laws, to undercut them in any way possible — like a cruel wind whistling around a hut to find a chink to penetrate. Since the 1920s their main hope had been some sort of manipulation in the name of women's rights. That this usually took the form of the E.R.A. proposal was due to the post–1920 possibility of an alliance with the "business and professional" feminists; it was not a necessity from the standpoint of the interests. From one viewpoint, Title VII had an advantage over the E.R.A. as an instrument because its positive side was helpful in disarming or confusing opposition. And it *had* a positive side.

A number of states jumped in alertly to use Title VII as a pretext for repealing their labor legislation for women completely. The pioneer state, which annulled all such laws in 1967, was Delaware — the very one that notoriously has a special relationship with corporation structures. A number of other states got rulings from their attorneys general stating that Title VII superseded the offending laws. Other states began amending their laws, sometimes in ways that would be satisfactory to labor — for example, in order to exempt women in supervisory situations. Some changes hit at the most vulnerable pieces of legislation, such as blanket restrictions on work hours and on weight-lifting.

What this meant for the most vulnerable women workers can be best described in the words of an authoritative voice for women trade-unionists, a trade-unionist who spoke out for tens of thousands of women whose labor representatives had been coopted by the Pure feminists just as many other union representatives had been coopted by management and its interests.

This was Myra Wolfgang, who, as we have seen,[6] was no flaming radical. An officer of the Hotel and Restaurant Employees Union, she had been a long-time admirer of the Auto Workers' union (U.A.W.) and its militant past. Here the operative word is past. She was disheartened by what had happened to that union by now, including its abdication not only before the auto giants but before N.O.W. In her 1970 testimony on the Pure E.R.A. before the Senate Judiciary Committee, she presented a slice of history that rarely makes its way into print, especially a slice of reality about the assembly lines of Michigan.

Wolfgang's target was a claim by the Business and Professional Women's federation, made in one of their booklets, a claim which has been endlessly repeated by E.R.A.-feminist propaganda. The B.P.W. booklet stated that "the days of sweat shops and intolerable working conditions, in which exploitation of women workers went rampant, are largely passed. The notion that women are frail and require special protection is obsolete." This claim has been repeated by N.O.W., in *Ms* magazine, and in political orations, without the least semblance of a scientific investigation.

Wolfgang replied first with an *ad hominem* — or rather *ad feminam* — thrust: "The days of exploitation are not over for thousands of women workers among the domestics who work in the homes of the Business and Professional Women!!" She went on:

> They were not over for thousands of Michigan women who worked without the protection of the

State's hour limit laws during a three-year period
in 1967 and the beginning of 1968.

She set out a review of "what occurred in Michigan." It is a
paradigm of what happened to real workingwomen while they
were being told that "intolerable working conditions" were as
dead as the Ford company's goon squads.

> In the 1967 session, the Michigan Legislature
> passed a Senate Bill 199 which repealed Section 9
> of Act 285, the 10-hour day–54 hours per week
> hours law for women. The same session of the
> Legislature passed Senate Bill 225 establishing an
> Occupational Safety Standards Commission
> which was mandated to establish codes of
> occupational standards for the protection of "life,
> health and safety of employees" in all areas
> covered by Act 285 (proper ventilation, toilet
> facilities, adequate wash and dressing rooms,
> seats for females, safety devices, hours laws, etc.).

In March 1968 the state attorney general, Frank Kelley,
ruled that the new Bill 225 went into effect prior to the repealer,
Senate Bill 199. There was confusion. Wolfgang comments:

> Legislators from both houses confessed complete
> ignorance as to why conflicting bills were passed.
> They assumed "women" wanted overtime. The
> secrecy with which this legislation passed (no
> hearings, no floor discussion) leaves no doubt,
> somebody knew the full repercussions of the

repealer. The Y.W.C.A., the Council of Catholic Women, the Council of Jewish Women, and most major women's groups and unions cheered the Attorney General's decision to reinstate the 54-hour maximum work week for women.

With this reinstatement of the maximum work week—

> the Women's Department of the U.A.W. dropped all pretense of wanting protective hours legislation for both men and women and blatantly offered to join the employers of Michigan in upsetting the Attorney General's opinion.

"This," added Wolfgang, "came as a complete shock to me since I am an admirer of that union." The U.A.W.'s shocking position was sent to the employers by the union's legal department, which told the employers: "We stand ready to give you whatever assistance we can in that endeavor" — the endeavor being the destruction of hours limitations for women workers.

That destruction was accomplished by the state Occupational Safety Standards Commission, which, after holding hearings, issued a regulation repealing the hours limitation laws for women.

> Then [related Wolfgang] the women of Michigan really became incensed, swung into action and formed an Ad-Hoc Committee Against Repeal of Protective Legislation. An outpouring of support came from [the ranks of] all major women's

organizations, church groups and labor unions, including many U.A.W. local unions. Thousands of women signed petitions urging the reinstituting of the hours law and supported litiga=tion started to request the court to restrain the Occupational Safety Standards Commission from repealing the hours law.

The suit was started by Stephanie Prociuk, a worker at the Hamtramck Division of Dodge, a U.A.W. shop steward and local committeewoman, the sort of militant in the ranks of this union that had once gained it the admiration of people like Myra Wolfgang. She had 33 years' seniority; she was single; she was the sole support of, and nurse to, her 81-year-old invalid father. Her testimony before the court made clear that the new regulation meant that Dodge could force overtime on her; that the forced labor of involuntary overtime would do "irreparable damage" to her and 200,000 other women represented by the Ad-Hoc Committee.

Her testimony [to return to Wolfgang's account] revealed that Dodge *did just that* while the law was thought to be inapplicable in the late fall and winter of 1967–68. During that period, she testified, she was called upon to work 69 hours a week: six days at 10 hours; on Sunday the company relented and had her work only 9 hours.

There were personal complications in this case: "She testified that forced overtime kept her from properly caring for her father, causing her undue worry and concern. She said she

124

could not afford either a nurse or housekeeper, did her own housework, including her laundry" — in addition to the 69 hours, of course. How unusual were such "complications"? Wasn't it true that a very large proportion of women had "complications" of one sort or another? She saw the "complications" about her at work:

> She testified that women dropped out with fatigue and exhaustion and had to be removed by stretcher. This, gentlemen, took place in 1968 — not at the turn of the century! ... She said her union was powerless to do anything about it and that the women's department of the union [U.A.W.] actually opposed any law "favoring women only."

Consider some typical "complications."

○ Prociuk's testimony was followed by that of a Chrysler worker, who told the same story about hours worked in accordance with Chrysler decrees. Her case was "complicated" too, of course: she was a widow with two daughters, aged 7 and 11, and a son of 9. She did all her own housework and had been on ADC before working at Chrysler. When the company was freed to lengthen the hours, it forced her to work 63 hours a week. She had no car, took two busses to get to work, and said that after three weeks on this forced schedule she became "sick in mind and body." If the hours limitation was destroyed, she would "have to quit work and go back on ADC." "Life is not worth living when you work like that," she said.

o Another witness, with 20 years' seniority in an auto factory, testified that her husband was totally disabled, and she was the sole support of the family (including an early teenage son). In addition to her factory hours, her responsibilities at home took four hours a day and all Saturday and Sunday. The extra money for overtime "wasn't worth it," she said. "It's like being on a merry-go-round in a nightmare — you don't know where you are or what time it is."

o Another witness, sole support of a disabled brother and a 67-year-old sister, said that "when the company could, they worked us 10 hours a day, six days a week, and 9 hours on Sunday." She *had* to work this 69-hour week, and she *had* to take care of the brother and sister, but the second imperative was of no interest to either the company or the highly principled feminists of the union...

o A witness employed at a meat-packing company reported that, when the hours limitation law was destroyed, "my boss ordered us to work 10 hours a day, seven days a week." She pointed out that this work was done "in a refrigerated room when the temperatures ranged from 32 to 40 degrees [Fahrenheit]" because it was meat that was wrapped.

After two days of this testimony, a circuit court judge ruled that the regulation repealing the hours limitation was invalid. Judge George T. Martin summed up the facts in favor of protecting women workers "against exploitation and hazard." While "some women" would cope, he said, "the great majority of working women feel that if they could not cope with additional overtime hours, they would be forced to either quit or else be fired and thereby suffer dire personal economic consequences."

The relief of "the great majority of women" was shortlived. At the end of 1969, the state attorney general, Frank Kelley, found a more effective ground for destroying the state's hours limitation for women workers. It was Title VII, and the E.E.O.C.'s guidelines for administering it. He issued an opinion, and lo, it was law.

The testimony about the real world — and real women — that had figured in the circuit court's hearing on the social problem was dismissed with a snap of Attorney General Kelley's opinion: "Since Michigan has no law limiting the number of hours a man may work, a woman is denied the same rights of overtime compensation as her male counterpart in direct violation of the Federal Act." Plainly, Mr. Kelley was exercised about women's equality, was he not? — though he had not previously been one of the paladins of women's rights. Let us note also that his opinion gave short shrift to the repeated assurances by E.R.A.-feminists that the effect of E.R.A. in such cases would be to extend good laws against exploitation to men as well as women. This "extension to men" solution did not warrant two words from the good attorney general.

Under the aegis of Title VII, as its potentialities unfolded, the climate hanging over the fate of women's labor legislation became that of a rout. Laws benefitting workingwomen were clubbed down on all sides, in state after state, to the accompaniment of triumphant cries from the business and professional feminists and the Pure philosophers of equality.

When the Illinois telephone company smashed the state's eight-hour work-day restriction, it explained with laudable candor that it saved money by paying women for overtime rather than hiring additional workers; nor did it claim to be motivated by enthusiasm for Justice. The women who were *not* employed as a result of this feminist "victory" existed only as statistics; they could not be asked how they liked it.

When a state's attorney general ruled the state's hours laws out of existence, and some auto and meat-packing plants made women work as much as 70 hours a week and more, many of these women had to leave their jobs — so their unions reported. It is not recorded that this fact bothered the type of feminist who could wax indignant only over the failure of the same companies to upgrade confidential secretaries into Board members and vice-presidents.

10 How the Pure E.R.A. Won — and Lost

Title VII constituted an unexpected flank attack on the body of women's labor legislation, coming at a point when labor's opposition to the Pure E.R.A. was at a low ebb.

The whole political climate had changed drastically. Self-consciously liberal tendencies (Americans for Democratic Action, for example) had faded away into mere letterhead organizations or less. Even the simulacrum of a socialist left dimmed out as radical sects stagnated and split themselves into cinders. The "silent generation" of youth and students offered little footing for feminist ideas.

Even the progressive side of the labor movement's hostility to the E.R.A. was diluted when the C.I.O. dissolved itself into the A.F.L. in the mid–fifties. The united AFL-CIO continued to oppose the E.R.A., to be sure, but typically with a greater infusion of the traditionalist motivation (which was the "safest" and most respectable stance). This traditionalist motivation sometimes entailed Male Supremacy notions (in the specific primitive-laborite form of the necessity for jobs for the Head of the Family) and objections to economic equality for women on job-trust grounds (since opening up trades to women disrupted the existing job-trust pattern).

The political clout of the AFL-CIO had started dwindling to where it is today, that is, to the lowest point in modern history. In this country it is rarely realized that its labor movement is one of the weakest and most impotent of any in the advanced industrial countries. The leaders of the A.F.L., and latterly of the AFL-CIO, liked to boast that they were "hardheaded pragmatists" interested only in immediate results, hence anti-revolutionary on principle, but in no comparable country was there such an astronomical gap between its objective strength in numbers and its political influence over the ruling parties even for bread-and-butter goals. Even its objective strength, in terms of percentage of unionized labor, has now dropped to only 19 percent.

In short, at no other time in this century has Congress been able with such impunity to disregard noises made by organized labor. At the same time, by the end of the 1960s and the beginning of the '70s, whatever still remained of a selfstyled radical movement had fragmented into splinters consisting of sectarians or crackpots, all of them alien to the interests of workingmen and workingwomen. The neofeminist movement that emerged as the dust rose from this wreckage had virtually no memory of, and no living connection with, the social-feminism of the past or (still less) with the older socialist feminism. This neofeminist movement industriously repeated the false claim that women's labor legislation was no longer an issue.

Now that labor had made itself a political nonentity under George Meany and his successors, now that radicalism existed mainly in discredited shards, and now that social-feminism was down the Memory Hole, the conditions were all set for the passage of the Pure E.R.A. by Congress in the 1970s.

In 1970 the strategists of the Pure E.R.A. decided to veer from the 1950–1953 pattern — by attacking first in the House of Representatives, not the Senate. The great new advantage was that the House debate would take place under rules that did not permit making amendments to the E.R.A. resolution. The proposal was now cast in the form of a parliamentary ultimatum: Pure or nothing.

The new floor manager in the House, successor to Katherine St. George of Tuxedo Park, was Representative Martha Griffiths of Michigan. She was a member of the Detroit Business Women's Club, and a favorite keynote speaker at gatherings of the Business and Professional Women's federation. When in 1971 she gave the keynote address at the B.P.W.'s national convention, she gave complete credit to the businesswomen for getting the E.R.A. passed in the House in 1970. The B.P.W. president introduced her with the organization's seal of approval: "Martha Griffiths is one of our own, a career woman and long-time B.P.W. member." It is unlikely that Stephanie Prociuk would have considered Griffiths as one of *her* own.

The Democratic machine men who controlled the Judiciary Committee, chaired by Celler of New York, followed the strong-arm tactic of simply bottling the E.R.A. resolution up in committee, without holding hearings. Griffiths bypassed this maneuver with another: a discharge petition to get the measure out on the floor. This move was successful because it not only had the support of the Republican leadership but also got a benevolent nod from the Democratic Party command in the House, who were not allied with Celler.

When the debate started on August 10, the Republican Party leader in the House was as strong a proponent of the Pure E.R.A. as William F. Knowland had been. He was Gerald R. Ford, who was destined for greater things, but was already well known as a rockribbed and rockheaded conservative. As such, Ford not only made an enthusiastic speech in favor of the Pure E.R.A., but attempted to put the sign of the Republican Party on the measure: he boasted of his mobilization of Republican stalwarts to sign the discharge petition. The Pure E.R.A. was still the protégé of the Republican Party's top leadership.

Gerald Ford particularly expressed his gratification that the House was acting on an E.R.A. "free and clear of anything like the Senate's Hayden rider." A South Carolina congressman took the occasion to needle those who thought that civil rights for blacks were more important than Justice for Women (meaning the E.R.A.); he chortled that "The day of capitulating to the like of the Black Panthers is over; the time for rewarding loyal

Americans is at hand." (One wonders what he had been told about just *who* was being rewarded by the new constitutional amendment.) A congressman from Delaware, which is sometimes confused with the state of Dupont, openly rested the case for the E.R.A. on improving the possibilities for "career businesswomen" to get ahead.

The House illustrated why it had the reputation of being more unbuttoned than the August Senate. But there was no difference when it came to bureaucratic procedures, on both sides. As mentioned, Celler had tried to head the E.R.A. off at the pass by ambushing it in committee. Once it was out in the open, the pro-E.R.A. forces not only outlawed amendments, but jammed it through *in a scant hour or so of alleged debate.* It was more like a brawl between opposing gangs of strong-arm men.

Even so, despite this blinding speed seldom seen in the capital, there were at least two alternatives suggested as against the Pure E.R.A. Their rejection serves to shed more light on just what was motivating the majority.

(1) The liberal-prolabor wing in the House, such as it was, counterposed the aim of implementing the recommendations submitted at the end of 1969 by the Presidential Task Force on Women's Rights and Responsibilities. The ease with which this serious report got lost in Washington, while the Pure E.R.A. was adopted in a scramble, testifies to the real concerns of the majority. The Task Force's recommendations listed a series of long-advocated aims of the women's movement. President Nixon — who, remember, lost no opportunity to boast of his support of the E.R.A. — submitted *no* legislative proposals to implement any of its recommendations.

Representative Mikva (Dem., Illinois), who was one of the House sponsors of the E.R.A., had in June introduced a Women's Equality Act. It was not at all counterposed to the E.R.A. It was necessary, he argued quite unanswerably, even if the E.R.A. were voted in. But this only presents us the pattern we have seen throughout: few of the House orators who demanded the instant adoption of the Pure E.R.A. showed any interest in anything so damnably concrete as the provisions of the Mikva bill.

(2) There was another futile attempt to combine good points of the E.R.A. with the interests of workingwomen, and it deserves special notice here because it points ahead. Representative Patsy Mink (Dem., Hawaii) had been a sponsor of the Mikva bill and knew what was involved. During the House scramble to adopt the E.R.A. resolution, she stood up to remind that there was a problem of good labor legislation for women, legislation that the E.R.A. should not be allowed to destroy.[1]

Therefore she suggested that the E.R.A. should have the following codicil added:

> *Provided,* That any State or Federal law which confers rights, benefits and privileges on one sex only shall be construed to apply to both sexes equally.

The Pure E.R.A. advocates had no basis for opposing this codicil, because it merely made explicit what *they* sometimes claimed (falsely) was implicit in the amendment. Patsy Mink pointed out that this language avoided all possible objections to the Hayden addition; it would *extend* women's protection to men also, on equal terms.

For those whose agenda was women's rights, the proposal was unanswerable. For those whose agenda looked more in the direction of destroying *existing* protective legislation, this proposal was a veritable horror — it not only did not destroy, it multiplied the existing legislation!

No one in the House picked it up. Patsy Mink herself did not push it. She told the House that floor manager Griffiths had assured her the amendment was not needed. (This was the hidden falsehood, passed around mostly orally, that the effect of the E.R.A. *would* be to extend protective legislation to men. It was believed, despite constant evidence to the contrary, mainly by people who wanted to believe it very much.) So Patsy Mink said she would vote for the E.R.A. resolution anyway. And anyway — all amendments were formally out of order, remember!

The House of Representatives passed the E.R.A. resolution by the vote of 352 to 15, with 62 not voting.[2] The *Washington Star* called it "the amazing one-hour feat of putting across an amendment pending for 47 years..."[3] The *New York Times* called it "an exercise in political opportunism,"[4] and conjectured that the reason many Congressmen voted for it was that they knew it did not have a chance in the Senate.*

The Senate took the E.R.A. up on October 7, in an extended debate that was going to have a peculiar dénouement. This was not a replay of 1953.

By now there was a distinct shift in the lineup. Missing was the sort of liberal-prolabor bloc of Senators that had been so prominent in the 1950s and before. The role that had been played in 1946 by Senator Robert Wagner and in 1950–1953 by Senator

---

* The voting statistics are taken from the House of Representatives website; they differ slightly from the numbers in the online version of the October 13 *Times* article. The west coast edition have had the correct numbers.

Herbert Lehman was now played by no one, symbolizing the political nullity of the AFL-CIO in the era of George Meany.

Accordingly, the dominant tone of the anti-E.R.A. forces shifted. We have pointed out that there were two allied, but quite different, currents opposing the Pure E.R.A. from two different sides: the liberal-labor objections to the Pure thing, and the traditionalists' objections. *Now it was the second of these that became dominant,* not only in men's minds but in overt discussion. The change was marked above all by this fact: it was not the Hayden addition that was now the spearhead of the opposition, but rather a significantly different amendment devised by Senator Sam Ervin, a conservative and racist Democrat from North Carolina.*

The fact that labor pressure on the Democratic Party was now weak made it easier for Democrats to take a more prominent role in the Pure E.R.A. drive. Unlike previous years, the alliance of businesswomen and corporate influence was able to put together a front that was more publicly bipartisan, not so much dominated by the Republicans as before. The feminist aura provided by organizations like N.O.W. helped too. The floor manager for the E.R.A. resolution was now Birch Bayh, a Democrat and a liberal by repute. The Democrats' majority leader, Mike Mansfield, cooperated with the Republicans in facilitating Senate action.

Perhaps out of self-confidence, Republican leader Hugh Scott allowed himself the unusually candid statement that the purpose of adopting the E.R.A. was to destroy the existing state laws protecting women:

---

* A few years later Ervin became a national celebrity as chairman of the Senate's Watergate investigation. Ervin's effectiveness in the anti-Nixon process rested on his known conservatism as well as on his reputation as a constitutional-law expert.

These State laws are the reason the equal rights amendment has been introduced in Congress after Congress. These State laws are the reason it must be adopted during this Congress.

The shift of the opposition toward the traditionalist approach was expressed in the debate both in content and procedure.

In the first place, Senator Ervin's main amendment went as follows:

This article shall not impair, however, the validity of any law ... which exempts women from compulsory military service or which is reasonably designed to promote the health, safety, privacy, education, or economic welfare of women, or to enable them to perform their duties as homemakers or mothers.

The main shift from the Hayden addition was represented by the first and last clauses. Just as the Hayden formula had been designed to keep some traditionalist support, so also the Ervin version included phrases to appeal to the labor motivation. But it was clear from Ervin's speeches that traditionalist sexism was his main thrust.

Ervin stressed in a warning to his colleagues that "it is inconceivable" that three-quarters of the state legislatures would ratify an amendment as sweeping and unmeasurable in its effect on sex roles as the Pure E.R.A. It is easy to see in hindsight that his foresight on this point had been well-founded. In effect, he was pointing to the dead weight of conservative and sexist feelings on the subject that would have to be over-come.

It is probable that a considerable number of the Senators who were going to vote yea knew this just as positively as Ervin. We have already mentioned the belief (which the *New York Times* had even put down in print) that it was possible for some to vote for the E.R.A. in Congress because of their secure knowledge that it was bound to fail in the states; hence they could tap the "women's vote" with impunity. (By this "women's vote" they meant the Pure E.R.A. faction, at this juncture.) Available to them, or to others, was also the constitutional theory, pushed by the E.R.A. proponents, that a vote for the amendment in Congress did not entail supporting it in the states.

The tactics of the opposition fragmented into piecemeal potshots. To begin with, Ervin abstracted the ban on compulsory military service for women which led off his amendment, and this issue became the focus of a separate debate and a separate vote. On October 13 this part of the Ervin formula was carried by a close vote, 36 to 33, with 31 not voting. Later that day, the Senate adopted a *real* rider, that is, a provision on a *different* subject (voluntary prayer in schools) that was tacked onto the E.R.A. resolution.

These unwelcome developments broke the nerve of the E.R.A. Senatorial managers. They now decided, and told the Senate, that the Pure E.R.A. had no chance.

The next day, the floor manager, Senator Birch Bayh, rose on the floor to make a *new* proposal on how to achieve equal rights for women. The story of this proposal, its content and its fate, deserves our closest scrutiny. It sheds a bright light on the whole issue, especially because the very existence of this alternative route was soon to be dropped down the Memory Hole like so many other aspects of our story.

11 On the Fourteenth Route

On October 14, 1970, Senator Birch Bayh, still speaking as the senatorial floor manager of the Pure E.R.A., made a remarkable announcement on the floor. He revealed that, despairing of success for the Pure amendment, he now pro-posed to take a different route to the same objective. He re-marked that *he was making this announcement without having first come to an agreement with the women's organizations he had been working with.*

The new proposed route, he suggested, should be an equal rights amendment which would no longer use the well-known language but, instead, *use the language of the "equal protection" clause of the Fourteenth Amendment* — in order to achieve exactly the same purpose of outlawing discrimination based on sex.

It was not a new idea, as we will see; but Senator Bayh was proposing a new way of implementing the idea, as an alternative to the Pure formula hitherto pushed in Congress. His discussion of this alternative, and the discussion by others, will provide us with new insights into the lineup on the issue, particularly into the thinking of those people who insisted on the Pure language or nothing.

The background of Bayh's proposal was the long history of feminists' disappointment with the failure of the Supreme Court to apply the Fourteenth Amendment to sex discrimination, as effectively as it had historically been applied against race discrimination.

For the language of the Fourteenth is *not* couched in terms of race; it refers to all "citizens" and all "persons," both terms including women without a shadow of a doubt. The operative clause of Section 1 of the amendment provides that "No State shall ... deny to any person within its jurisdiction the equal protection of the laws." There is no more reason, in the language of the amendment, to apply this to all sexes than to all races — and no less reason, too.

The history of Supreme Court decisions has been that this injunction (not "deny to any person ... the equal protection of the laws") has been applied to cases of discrimination committed against "persons" on account of race, but it has not been applied to cases of discrimination committed against (female) persons on account of their sex.

The convolutions of the legal mind which were devised to justify this byzantine conclusion need not delay us, but let no one think that the decisive reason was the question of Congressional intention. It happens that a clause in both the Fourteenth and the Fifth Amendments offers the premier example of how the court interpreted the Constitution *without* being obsessed by legislative intention. This example concerns precisely the meaning of "person."

The well-known "due process" clause was applied by the court, in a twist of legal thinking, to a "person" quite unknown to the Founding Fathers, namely, to the brand-new kind of legal "person" known as a *corporation.* In contrast, no twist was necessary to include women under the rubric of "persons"; women are commonly conceded to be such, even by traditionalists. But the Supreme Court refused to apply the guarantees of the Fourteenth Amendment to this kind of person, while a juridical fiction covered corporations with the guarantees of American Freedom, as if they were human beings.

Pro-E.R.A. leaders had long conceded that the Fourteenth Amendment could do the job, if the Supreme Court permitted it to do so.

The idea had even come up in the National Woman's Party, though it will be instructive to see what happened to it. Back in 1938, it was suggested by a leading member of what by then was a very tiny N.W.P. group: Ethel Adamson, of the New Jersey organization, national chair of the party's Susan B. Anthony Memorial Committee (which had some importance in the group at that time). Adamson conducted a small campaign among the N.W.P. leadership in favor of a test-case approach to expanding the coverage of the Fourteenth Amendment to cover sex discrimination. She wrote to Alice Paul on December 22 of that year:

I have been thinking over this fundamental principle
of women being in the Constitution and wondering if
now — in these more advanced times — there could
be obtained a decision by the Supreme Court which
would declare women to be PERSONS.

This would take care of the opposition's arguments, she thought
(quite justifiably):

If we could bring MEN under all *protective*
legislation equally with women that would do away
with protective legislation in its objectionable
features.

Such an effort "might possibly give us our equal rights without
the expense and labor of a campaign for the Amendment." At a
minimum "it might give much publicity and talking points, and keep
the matter before the public as a *Cause Célèbre* in the Supreme
Court." Besides, her argument went on, this course did not necessarily
take the place of an E.R.A.; we could get both more easily:

If we could get [such] a decision of the Supreme
Court ... that would end many of the injustices to
women. If we still wanted a special Amendment for
Equal Rights — which sentimentally really should
occupy a special place for itself in the Constitution, it
might be very easy to achieve *after* a Supreme Court
decision had practically made such an enactment
valid and compulsory.[1]

Adamson wrote also to other leaders of the group.

Alice Paul could not be bothered. She asked the party's Campaign Secretary, Caroline L. Babcock, to respond to Adamson. Babcock dismissed the suggestion in a short note which utterly failed to confront the main points that Adamson had made:

> Miss Paul says that it seems to her that it is better to go on with the idea of getting an Amendment to the Constitution because the work of getting such an Amendment through Congress and through the States creates a body of opinion in its favor; that it does not seem to her useful or possible to pass an amendment like the equal rights amendment without developing that body of favorable opinion.[2]

This ignored Adamson's point that a favorable Supreme Court action could stimulate and facilitate "the work of getting such an Amendment." In fact, Paul's view is perilously close to an attitude that critics had charged to her: that in her mind the E.R.A. was simply a peg on which to hang a party-building campaign, if not activism-for-the-sake-of-activism. The letter communicating Paul's view continued as follows: "A Supreme Court's decision would not have this effect, she thinks" (though she gave no reasons) "and it could always be reversed." (As we will see, this point about reversability was answered by Bayh's proposal.)

Ethel Adamson seems to have backed down when she received Alice Paul's brush-off, and the N.W.P. *Papers* do not show that further consideration was given in its ranks to the idea of the Fourteenth Amendment route.

But the idea continued to hang in the air. Earlier in 1970, Representative Griffiths, the E.R.A. floor manager in the House, even told the lower chamber that she felt her battle was with the Supreme

Court. "All this amendment [the E.R.A.] asks," she said, "could easily be done without the amendment, if the Supreme Court were willing to do it, but they are not." She not only conceded but emphasized that the E.R.A. was necessary only because of the court's failure to interpret the Fourteenth properly.

Senator Bayh's proposal was' to use the *language* of the Fourteenth Amendment in a *new* amendment which would state outright and positively that it covered sex discrimination. It is obvious immediately that this negated the common argument (used by Alice Paul *inter alii*) that a Supreme Court decision might be reversed. Bayh's idea combined all the advantages of using the Fourteenth's language together with none of the drawbacks.

True, there had been some change in the court's posture that had become visible over the years. Senator Bayh himself referred to this, as being encouraging but insufficient in itself. He argued that his new amendment "would make it absolutely clear" that Congress and the states did not agree with the traditional course taken by the Supreme Court, that is, its refusal to apply the Fourteenth to sex. "Many scholars have contended that these [court] decisions were likely to fall, in time, in any case. The Court's 14th Amendment standards have evolved dramatically in recent time. But this [new] amendment would remove any doubt whatsoever..."

And a little later: yes, "We have made considerable progress. Especially in the last few years the courts have taken great strides toward providing the kind of equality I believe is necessary." However: "The Supreme Court still has a long way to go..." But there is no reason, Bayh argued, to wait until the Supreme Court caught up with the world.

> I believe that if given enough time the Court would
> eventually hold that the Equal Protection Clause of

the 14th Amendment demands the kind of equality between the sexes which the equal rights amendment would guarantee. But that process would take far too long in my judgment.[3]

What about the opposing general, marshaling the Senate forces opposed to the E.R.A., namely, Senator Ervin? In a remarkable development, Ervin expressed his belief that the Fourteenth Amendment could make the E.R.A. unnecessary, that "the Equal Protection Clause, properly interpreted, nullifies every state law lacking a rational basis which seeks to make rights and responsibilities turn upon sex."[4]

Both sides were for the Fourteenth route to sex equality, both floor managers said they would accept the language of the Fourteenth as the way to eliminate sex discrimination! What was there to fight about?

One of the leading legal authorities commonly put forward by the Pure E.R.A. forces, Professor Leo Kanowitz, likewise put considerable hope in the Fourteenth route. He presented a weighty paper to the Senate Judiciary Committee just before the 1970 debate, and it was even inserted in full into the *Congressional Record* by the E.R.A.'s supporters.[5] Kanowitz pointed out that nowadays the Supreme Court does concede that the Fourteenth applies to women; the court has merely argued that "women in many situations constitute a class that can reasonably be subjected to separate treatment." This view leaves the door open to laws that are formulated in terms of sex differentiation.

And Kanowitz stated flatly that the adoption of the E.R.A. "would not fundamentally change the picture" with regard to this court interpretation. There is nothing in the one-sentence blast of the E.R.A., any more than in the Fourteenth Amendment, that would cause the courts to *cease* to permit "sex classifications ... if it can be demonstrated that though they are expressed in terms of sex, they are in reality based on function."

This opinion, which is not peculiar to Kanowitz but which is common among constitutional lawyers, will come as a surprise to victims of the propaganda blitz, who have been told thousands of times that the E.R.A. is Pure precisely because of its brevity. We will see below that this vaunted brevity is precisely what makes the E.R.A. a paper tiger, and that the only sure consequence of the E.R.A. is a symbolic feeling of satisfaction and not a positive legal impact.

Kanowitz was of the opinion, then, that the language of the E.R.A. does not exclude sex classifications based on function in the courts' opinion; that it would not illegalize sex-discriminatory laws any more thoroughly than would the Fourteenth Amendment. But Kanowitz was in favor of the E.R.A. Why then?

The passage of the E.R.A., he explained, would demonstrate "an unshakable *intention"* to eliminate sex discrimination; it "would give *encouragement"* to the reformers, and otherwise provide the *symbolic* impetus to virtue. (Italics added.) To which we must add, lest it be forgotten: for this encouraging symbol, juridically dubious in content, workingwomen have to let hard-won working conditions be taken away from them in far from symbolic fashion.

Professor Kanowitz added a caution about a danger — a danger that was going to take on some substance. Congress, in adopting an E.R.A., must make clear in its legislative record that it still encouraged the Supreme Court to interpret the Fourteenth in an antisexist way.

> I say this because there is a very real danger that if
> this is not done, the adoption of an amendment at this
> time will ultimately represent a defeat rather than a

victory for those of us who seek the eradication of irrational sex-based distinctions in American law and society.

Because the court may reason this way: since Congress has deemed it necessary to adopt a new amendment, it must have believed that nothing else in the Constitution provides relief. This reasoning may tend to stop the court from continuing to modify its traditional Fourteenth position, pending E.R.A. ratification. In the interim the needed clarification may come to a halt.

Here is where we come out: for the sake of the symbolic act of "encouragement" etc., which is alleged to be sufficient ground to support the E.R.A., we get two hard-edged real consequences — not only the destruction of the remaining state labor legislation, but also a damper on the process of relief from the dangers of sex classification itself.

This should help us to understand the cogency and appeal of the new equal-rights amendment which Senator Bayh pro-posed on October 14: "Neither the United States nor any State shall on account of sex, deny to any person within its jurisdiction the equal protection of the laws." This, if adopted, would put the Fourteenth's language into immediate and full operation *without* waiting for the uncertain evolution of the Supreme Court.

Senator Bayh's presentation speech demonstrated that the new (Fourteenth-type) wording of the amendment got around the reasonable objections that had been made to the old one-sentence blast, while still doing what he wanted an E.R.A. to do. He agreed that "the precise language" of the old amendment has no "special magic," and that perhaps it needed revision in any case, given the "dramatic evolution in our concepts of constitutional equality." As an example of the kind of fundamental objection which it answered, he cited the argument against the E.R.A. made by Professor Paul Freund of the Harvard Law School —

> who takes the position that "not every legal differentiation between boys and girls, men and women, husbands and wives, is of" an "obnoxious character, and that to compress all these relationships into one tight little formula is to invite confusion, anomaly, and dismay."

Thus Bayh strongly agreed that a requisite degree of "flexibility" had to be built into an equal rights amendment. He even insisted that the old E.R.A. did have such flexibility (unlike the rigid interpretations of the N.W.P. doctrinaires), and he cited his — and Representative Griffiths' — opinion that the Pure E.R.A. *would* allow legal discrimination between the sexes in cases of "overriding and compelling public interest."*

In any case, the necessary flexibility, he thought, was rendered without doubt by the new amendment, which recognized "the need for a flexible standard in cases where different treatment under the law may be justified."

A big fact about the Fourteenth route was that there was a long-tested body of law around the Equal Protection clause, whereas the new language of the Pure amendment would have to *begin* building up a body of interpretive law through a period (undoubtedly a long one) of litigation and lawsuits. Birch Bayh argued that his new idea

---

* This point gives much of the game away for the Pure E.R.A. A team of horses could be driven through the hole opened up by this formulation. Most of the naive supporters of the Pure amendment have been propagandized to believe that not a word in it must be changed precisely in order to avoid such flexibility, that is, they believe the amendment is clear simply because it is so bare and laconic. But it is these and similar statements by the Congressional managers of the E.R.A. that lay down the legislative record conditioning the meaning that the Pure E.R.A. will be given by the courts; and the thousands of contrary statements by N.O.W. and *Ms* magazine (or by Professor Thomas Emerson of Yale) have only propaganda value.

would harness the cause of sex equality to the existing body of law, the same body of law that had been built up to implement the banning of race discrimination.

In the following important passage of his speech, Senator Bayh stated the juridical advantage of his new approach:

> ... the [new] amendment would clearly prevent the kind of restrictive interpretation and disruptive application which the critics have feared. By relying upon the language of the Equal Protection Clause, the amendment would incorporate a vast body of experience in dealing with the most difficult questions of discrimination. The standards of application under the 14th Amendment have developed into a coherent and comprehensive body of law. ... There can be no doubt that this amendment would assure the kind of continuity and consistency for which the opponents of [the old E.R.A.] have been arguing.

The layman, perhaps bedazzled by the illusory simplicity of the Pure E.R.A., may not appreciate one aspect of this argument. We have not yet done justice to a side of the Congressional debates which sounds technical-juridical when it is read in the dull pages of the *Congressional Record* but which may have an overriding influence on the courts.

More than once it was demonstrated that the most responsible advocates of the Pure amendment broke down and admitted that *they did not know* what the juridical impact of their amendment would be on specific areas of law. Lay people may be unconcerned about this area of uncertainty. But for a chamber of Congress filled with rather skilled lawyers, it was another matter. For these lawyers, and for anyone else concerned about the juridical meaning of the Pure one-sentence blast, Senator Bayh's new formula performed an important ser-vice: it swept a number of juridical problems away. Bayh could say, and did say, that the whole minutely worked-out body of judicial experience that had been applied to *racial* discrimination via the Fourteenth route — all this could now be shifted over, practically in one piece, to do the same job for sex discrimination.

To be sure, as everyone knows, the Fourteenth Amendment did not really root out all racial discrimination; it confined this discrimination, at best. But in truth Senators like Bayh, who faced the facts, expected no more than that from the Pure E.R.A., at the best; and he hoped for no less. As we have seen, knowledgeable theoreticians of law like Professor Kanowitz hoped mainly that the E.R.A. would provide a *symbolic* demonstration of "intention" and "encouragement." Bayh came to the same point with his paramount argument for the amendment:

> ... most important, this amendment would retain the
> most essential benefit of the equal rights amendment
> — the extraordinary symbolic value of a national
> mandate in the area of discrimination on account of
> sex.

While the managers of the movement in Congress thought of the E.R.A. as mainly a "symbol," the rank and file of the women's organizations were still being told that the Pure amendment would sweep away all sex discrimination with one iron broom. The gap in thinking shown here was going to grow bigger in the future, not smaller.

With the presentation of Senator Bayh's new amendment — a newly proposed E.R.A. by the current Senatorial floor manager — it might have seemed that the E.R.A. problem had at last been resolved.

As we have seen, even the opposing floor manager, Senator Ervin, was indicating his benign interest. Logically, Ervin would *have* to support the Bayh formula; on the basis of his previous statements and argumentation, it is hard to see what sort of case he could make against it. As for traditionalist-sexist opponents of the E.R.A. in any form, it is true that some might continue to oppose it, but these would have to come out into the open by making the traditionalist viewpoint the focus of Senate consideration *for the first time in this debate;* and most of *them* would be reluctant to do so. Anyway, in that case they could be more easily isolated.

The liberal-prolabor bloc of Senators appeared to be lining up in favor of the new Bayh formula. They had obviously been approached by Bayh before he made his announcement. Bayh was immediately succeeded on the floor by the Republican liberal-prolabor senator from New York, Jacob Javits, who fervently endorsed the new proposal, emphasizing that he did so as a previous supporter of the Pure E.R.A. Bayh's comanager of the E.R.A. in the Senate, Senator Marlow Cook, told the chamber he was a cosponsor of the new amendment.

An even more telling scene was acted out in the House, which (remember) had already adopted the Pure E.R.A. formula. Here the amendment's manager, Representative Griffiths, stated flatly that "I have been pleased to join with Senators Bayh, Kennedy, Javits, Goodell, Cook and Dole" in sponsoring the new amendment. The mention of Senator Edward Kennedy's name as a sponsor was new, again assuring a realignment in favor of the Bayh formula. Griffiths was saying that she was ready to get the Pure E.R.A. *replaced* with the Fourteenth formula in the House, if the Senate acted on it. Indeed, she had already worked closely with Senator Bayh in working up the proposal, and an assistant to Bayh recalled that she was "enthusiastic" about the new route.[6]

That was one side of the new development. The reader cannot fail to recall that there was another side: *what was the meaning of the new Fourteenth route for the much-desired destruction of women's labor legislation?* Would the new Bayh formula have the same impact in this regard — or more? or less?

One of the outstanding differences between the Pure sentence and the Fourteenth language, a difference that was quite out in the open, was this: the Fourteenth formula could be reconciled with legislation benefitting women, in certain cases and contexts. This was evident from the juridical history that had already accumulated about this language of the Fourteenth. The adoption of the Fourteenth route would have all of the "symbolic" value that everyone talked about, but it would not *preclude* all prowoman legislation. The latter issue would still have to be fought out, measure by measure, by anyone who wanted to fight about it.

This put the spotlight strongly on the central question about the whole fight: in the case of this, that or the other proponent of the Pure E.R.A., was the motive really that of encouraging women's rights, or was it the destruction of labor legislation? Senator Bayh, for example, obviously thought it was the former motivation; and we would venture the opinion that the second did not occur to him — until it hit him over the head a few days later.

The whole promising new development of a new E.R.A. was quickly and thoroughly wrecked — by "the women," said Bayh. Which women?

By this time, we should make clear, the little group of doctrinaires around Alice Paul and the National Woman's Party had dwindled in importance and influence. The N.W.P. played little or no role in the blowup of the Fourteenth route, though the group held the same views as those who did the blowing-up.

Bayh had to deal with the bigger battalions of establishment "feminism." In the first place, this meant the organized women of the Republican and Democratic Party machines, who put their pressure on him as the Women's Committees of the major parties. Ancillary to these big guns were such organizations as the National Association of Women Lawyers (N.A.W.L.), the Citizen's Advisory Council on the Status of Women, and in large part also the National Federation of Business and Professional Women (B.P.W.) — though we will see that the last-named played a more reluctant role. Vocal, but with less impact, was the National Ad Hoc Committee for the E.R.A., an umbrella group of D.C. women's organizations led by Flora Crater.

Although N.O.W. pursued the same line to strike down the Fourteenth route, it was apparently considered not quite upper-bracket by the establishment women's battalions, and it tailed after the latter without being admitted to the anterooms of power. In any case, it was the front headed by the Republican/Democratic Party ladies that Bayh's initiative smashed into.[7]

Bayh had carefully given some of these key women advance notice of his intention to propose a substitute. On October 12, 1970, he had called representatives of the influential women's groups into his office. They included *inter alii* Marguerite Rawalt, a past president of the B.P.W. and subsequently a leading Washington lawyer representing the N.A.W.L.; Gladys O'Donnell of the National Federation of Republican Women; and Catherine East, Executive Secretary of the Citizen's Advisory Council. No one was present from N.O.W. at this meeting.

Bayh explained his intention and the difficulty of getting the E.R.A. passed in the current Congress; he showed a copy of the new proposal and asked for a "quick opinion." The women there expressed their opinion: thumbs down. But they wouldn't oppose his introduction of the new formula, they said (later explaining that this was due to the lack of time to stop him). Bayh was going to write to other women's organizations asking for opinions.

But without waiting, the Senator introduced the substitute amendment on October 14, as we saw, telling the chamber that he didn't know as yet "whether it will be satisfactory to the various women's groups who have worked so hard for passage of a constitutional amendment." We have seen no information showing that the conscientious Senator tried to check the question with any women's representatives speaking for workingwomen or trade-unionists.

This was not the first time, however, that Senator Bayh had tried to get his "key" women's organizations to let up on their stand of "Pure E.R.A.-or nothing." In previous months he had tried to do this through his legislative aide, Paul J. Mode, who was a lawyer.[8] According to Catherine East, he had been told, politely but firmly, "to go fly a kite." Their reaction this time was much the same.

Marguerite Rawalt and Catherine East forwarded the proposed Bayh substitute to their favorite pro-E.R.A. lawyer, Professor Thomas Emerson of Yale Law School. He initially told them the language was "okay," but later warned that the statements made on the Senate floor by Bayh and the Republican cosponsor Senator Marlow Cook, made in support of their new amendment, set a precedent for the continuation of the dreaded protective labor laws and other forms of special treatment for women. (Emerson's previous "okay" opinion simply showed he was not knowledgeable about the Fourteenth route.)

Alerted to the fact that the destruction of labor legislation was at stake, the women's organizations — those who re-presented "women" to the much-harassed Senator Bayh — went to work to kill the Fourteenth route. Their watchword was: better nothing at all. As Gladys O'Donnell, president of the National Federation of Republican Women, wrote Bayh in October: "We would prefer to see the E.R.A. go down to total defeat than to be glossed over with a gratuitous gesture."[9] This despite her knowing that E.R.A. advocates like Professor Kanowitz "glossed over" the Pure E.R.A. as mainly a "symbolic" reassurance...

Harriet Cipriani, O'Donnell's opposite number for the women of the Democratic National Committee, joined with O'Donnell to call a private meeting of reliable women's organizations on November 2 to get up a united front of establishment women to ensure the defeat of Bayh's Fourteenth route amendment. They wrote Senators Bayh and Cook of their intention, and made the Senators a noteworthy offer: this demarche would be kept secret from the press if the Senators would be so kind as to kill the amendment *themselves,* thereby avoiding political embarrassment:

> Following that [Nov. 2 meeting], we would hope to be able to delegate a small group to meet with you [Cook] and Senator Bayh to present a formal request that the Substitute Amendment be withdrawn. There will be no press release about this activity for we do not wish to embarrass anyone.[10]

Out of this November 2 meeting grew a "coordinating council" of women's organizations for the Pure E.R.A. The council was very busy in the next weeks, meeting frequently in the offices of the Republican Women in the Rayburn Congressional Office Building. But the first objective failed: Bayh and Cook refused to slink away quietly from the substitute amendment, an amendment which had already offered new hope to people on Capitol Hill who had thought that the E.R.A. issue was a hopeless tangle.

And so, on November 12, the leaders of "women" held a press conference to make known their consensus position against the Bayh amendment. Their press release stated very clearly who was bossing this operation:

> Such was the consensus of opinion at a joint organizational meeting sponsored by Gladys O'Donnell, President of the National Federation of Republican Women, and Harriet Cipriani, Deputy Vice-Chairman of the Democratic National Committee, called to discuss and consider the request of Senator Birch Bayh for views on his substitute proposal of October 14, 1970.[11]

The day after this press release, N.O.W. also issued a statement of outright opposition to the Bayh substitute. It did so at a press conference sponsored by Crater's Ad Hoc Coalition, a broader assemblage of women's groups than the council of the Republican and Democratic leaders.[12] N.O.W. rejected the Bayh substitute with exactly the same motivation as the battalions of Republican and Democratic women: viz., the substitute leaves room for women's labor laws. N.O.W.'s public statement concluded:

> N.O.W. opposes the Bayh substitute, however well intended it is, because it and its legislative history would establish Constitutional backing for existing discriminatory practices which continue under the guise of "protection" and which deprive women of

the right to make the same choices about their lives
that men do.[13]

Interestingly enough, while N.O.W. stood firm against the least
possibility of protective laws benefitting women workers, the Business
and Professional Women's federation wavered. (We have noted before
that this organization had a propensity for individual mavericks with
progressive inclinations.) Perhaps because of discouragement at the
Pure E.R.A.'s slow progress, a feeling also motivating Senator Bayh
himself, the then leaders of the B.P.W. told Senator Bayh to go ahead
with the Fourteenth route. A hostile observer has blamed their stand on
their close ties with Bayh himself.[14]

But among the women supporters of the Pure E.R.A., the
watchword was still "All or nothing." There was little inhibition about
putting it that way. Bayh's letter inviting opinions from women leaders
got this reply, for example, from Phyllis Wetherby of Pittsburgh's
N.O.W. organization, a research engineer for U. S. Steel and a
Democratic Committeewoman: "Yes, I do want all or nothing... .
[A]nything else will only encourage the continuance of discriminatory
'protections.' "[15]

On November 16 Bayh capitulated. He withdrew his substitute
amendment from Senate consideration. "There are differing opinions
about the proposal," he told the Senate. "I would like to have a chance
to discuss these differences personally with some of the leaders of
women's organizations in an effort to see if we cannot reconcile some
of the differences that exist."[16] Evidently he was saying that *he* was
unconvinced by the "all or nothing" position. Two days later he held
such a meeting, and there, faced by the same intransigence, he said he
would give up on the question until "next year."

Next year, back to the Pure E.R.A. That was the agenda. What
actually happened was not altogether Pure.

12 How They Snatched Defeat from the Jaws of Victory

The whole women's *Apparat* of the Republican and Democratic Parties had been mobilized to defeat the Bayh substitute amendment. This was the power before which Bayh had collapsed. That power certainly was not N.O.W., which had even been elbowed out of the managing "coordinating council" of the women's establishment organizations, but which added its voice against the substitute in its own statement. It was not the National Woman's Party, which was now barely existent as a splinter group.

When Bayh and Cook resumed their management of the E.R.A. in January 1971, Bayh, giving a legislative history of the proposal, pretended that the whole Fourteenth episode had never taken place. In his account to the Senate, that episode was as nonexistent as a Khrushchev speech in the then-current Kremlin textbook. It was down the Memory Hole, like so much of E.R.A. history.

From here on, the Pure amendment had clear sailing in Congress. If anyone thinks that this was so because the whole Senate and House of Representatives had been finally converted to women's equality in its purest form, this person is to be sincerely envied as a believer in miracles. To find out what was involved less miraculously, let us summarize the outcome.

The House took up the Pure amendment again on October 6, 1971. There was a last procedural flurry. The Judiciary Committee reported it out with an addition of its own, the so-called "Wiggins amendment," sponsored by Charles Edward Wiggins, Republican of California, which permitted exemption of women from compulsory military service, and also allowed for law "which reasonably promotes the health and safety of the people." The procedure was established so as to permit a choice only between this Wiggins amendment and the Pure formula. The Wiggins amendment was defeated 265 to 87. On October 12 the Pure E.R.A. was carried 354 to 24.

The Senate acted in March of 1972. A series of amendments by Senator Ervin failed to carry by votes averaging about 75 to 14. Then, on March 22, 1972, the pristine, unchanged Pure E.R.A. was adopted 84 to 8.

Does this mean that there were *only eight Senators* who were opposed to (say) compulsory military service for women? If anyone thinks so, we should like to interest this person in some California swampland for sale near a ring of chemical plants... As Professor Hewlett stresses, one interesting thing about the vote in Congress was its heterogeneity: "E.R.A. opponents were hard to come by. Hubert Humphrey was for it, and so was George Wallace. Bella Abzug rooted for it, but so did Spiro Agnew."[1]

We suggest that something else happened. It was not a conspiracy or a secret; it happened right on the record, and can be read in the *Congressional Record.*

We have mentioned what every constitutional lawyer knows: that in interpreting a new law, it is not only the bare words of the law that are illuminating, but what the judges call the "legislative record." This record is made on the floor of Congress by the proponents of the law. And when the "bare words of the law" are kept as bare and as few as in the Pure formula, the legislative record grows correspondingly in importance.

The debate in the House, where the amendment was taken up first, contributed heavily to the legislative record. The debate was noteworthy in this respect: it provided a powerful basis which would permit the courts to make various "sex classifications," as Professor Kanowitz and others had explained, in spite of the *apparent* rigidity of the one-sentence blast.

Representative Griffiths — who was once again the E.R.A. floor manager in the House — was confronted by Representative Charles Edward Wiggins with a loaded question. The question purported to show that, given the E.R.A., laws could still "make rational distinctions between persons on the basis of sex." Griffiths, not too happily, conceded that such distinctions could still be made "as may be generally related to their physical differences." *She* adduced rape laws as her example; but the courts would make their own applications of the principle conceded by the amendment's floor manager.

Wiggins stressed, with a plethora of evidence, that the supporters of the E.R.A. had great differences among them-selves on how they thought it would affect the legal system. Some, following the lead of a school of thought headed by Professor Emerson of Yale, proposed that "equal" must virtually always be interpreted as "identical," and that sex classifications were virtually outlawed. Others permitted "reasonable" classification, and there were extensive differences on what was considered reasonable. *What emerged from the discussion was that the Congressional managers of the E.R.A. belonged to the second school.* That means that *they* were determining how the courts would interpret the amendment's spare language, and that Professor Emerson's writings on the subject would be useful only for inspiring N.O.W. activists with illusions.

It should be remarked that Wiggins, in this last attempt to add a codicil to the E.R.A., emphasized that *his* amendment, unlike Hayden's, did not have the effect necessarily of safeguarding labor laws for women. This was an effort to narrow still more the distance between pro- and anti-E.R.A., until they merged like the images in a stereopticon.

Toward the end of the debate, floor manager Griffiths came out with an unusually strong statement for the "legislative record." We cannot reveal what happened behind the scenes because we do not know, and perhaps nothing happened there (outside of the usual informal conversations). But what is evident on the printed pages of the *Congressional Record* is that this statement must have consolidated support for the amendment. *For it told the Congress in perfectly clear language that the E.R.A. would be interpreted by the courts in exactly the same way as the Fourteenth route amendment.*

This was not a crystal-ball prediction; this was self-fulfilling. For by making this statement on the floor, and speaking as the spokesperson of the E.R.A. forces, Griffiths was telling the courts of the future how Congress wanted the "bare words" interpreted.

In this statement she stressed: it is not true that the E.R.A. can do anything more than can be done by an implementation of the Fourteenth Amendment.

> Oh no, Mr. Chairman, that is not true. The real truth is that the equal rights amendment, even if passed, might still be interpreted as the 14th amendment has been interpreted and give no rights to women. The 14th amendment has been interpreted to permit any classification that the Court deems reasonable...

> Mr. Chairman, what the equal rights amendment seeks to do, and all it seeks to do, is to say to the Supreme Court of the United States, "Wake up! This is the 20th century..."

With this extraordinary statement by the E.R.A.'s representative in the House, on the verge of the final vote, there is left little doubt how the amendment would be interpreted once on the books. The Pure bloc had demanded all or nothing; they had gotten all *and* nothing. Nothing except what could have been put into the law decades and decades before this.

In the House debate, one of Wiggins' supporters, J. Edward Hutchinson, Republican of Michigan, drew a striking conclusion from the situation. Our summary of his argument would go like this:

> The pro-E.R.A. people think they are avoiding a *piecemeal* approach to equal rights, avoiding the process of removing specific inequalities and abuses by specific measures. But in fact they are simply trading one piecemeal approach for another. They will be able to establish the concrete import of E.R.A. only by one court case after another, and specific inequalities and abuses will be ended only a case at a time.

But there is a big difference between the two piecemeal approaches: the forum in which it is pursued. The Pure E.R.A. means that forum will be *in the courts rather than in the legislatures.* Moreover, it will be in the federal courts, the one least reachable by the people in the first instance. And the history of the Supreme Court is a history of discovering meanings and powers in constitutional amendments that no one had previously dreamed of. Once the Pure single-sentence is un-leashed, its real meaning will become the sole province of the Supreme Court and no one else. Yet it is precisely because they distrusted the courts' interpretations in this field that Representative Griffiths et al. asked Congress for a constitutional amendment!

Such was Hutchinson's argument, put a little more directly than Hutchinson had done. Outside the Capitol, women's organizations were celebrating the passage of the E.R.A. as a famous victory. But as soon as one took a close look at the victory, peculiarities showed up. Unfortunately, since this was a proposed amendment and not merely another law, fifty other legislative bodies had to take a closer look, and hence about a hundred million women (not to speak of men) were further encouraged to do so. The result, as we know, was disastrous for the amendment.

It is no part of this book's aim to survey and analyze the reasons for the failure of the E.R.A. to get the required approval of two-thirds of the states. There is a comment to be made, however, in terms of the hidden history of the E.R.A., a consideration which emerges from the story told on these pages but which — by its nature — played no overt role.

First a summary of the facts. During the first year or so, 28 states ratified the amendment, but over the next nine years only seven more states added themselves to the list. The original seven-year ratification period expired with only 35 states giving their approval, out of the 38 required. Congress adopted an extension, whose legality was vigorously questioned, but by June 30, 1982, its deadline, it too had failed to save the amendment. Several states even reversed their earlier ratifications, or stated they wanted to do so. In 1975 the E.R.A.'s proponents were stunned (the word is not too strong) when New York and New Jersey voted against the adoption of state E.R.A.'s: for these were two states that had not only ratified the national amendment but were regarded as sure things by their strong feminist organizations.

It is very instructive to read the press productions of the pro-E.R.A. forces after the New York–New Jersey bombshell. No one had the least idea why this terrible development had taken place. It was an utter mystery. Then, in 1980, for the first time in over 35 years, the Republican Party dropped support of the E.R.A. from its platform. The Democratic Party leadership refused to back a convention-supported platform plank that would have ended party financial support to party candidates who refused to support the E.R.A.

If the reader wishes to penetrate this mystery, we have a suggestion: to begin with Professor Sylvia Hewlett's *A Lesser Life* and its chapter on "The E.R.A.: A Test Case." The least this will do is eliminate the conspiracy theory which was the main product of the E.R.A. thinkers; that is, the claim that it was all due to a right-wing-funded cabal in which the "Moral Majority" and similar troglodyte groups financed Phyllis Schlafly's campaign to "Stop E.R.A."

Hewlett gives Schlafly a great deal of credit (perhaps more than we would) for crystallizing the Stop E.R.A. sentiment, but she rightly puts the spotlight on *the grass-roots sentiment among American women which was there to be crystallized.* The mass of women were ready to believe that the E.R.A. was really a "men's liberation" measure, because they were brought to realize what they stood to lose. Their trade-union leaders, including most of the women leaders (who were oriented toward establishment-feminism), failed to tell them; Schlafly did, in the midst of her socially reactionary diatribes about "women's lib" atrocities.

Any explanation of the startling ratification fiasco that focuses solely or mainly on Schlafly misses the point. What hits the point is Hewlett's account of how and why she stopped working for E.R.A. ratification. It is a relatively short account, and the reader is requested to hold still to read it, remembering that Hewlett herself was utterly innocent of any link with or experience of the life of workingwomen.

Hewlett explains that, attending a meeting of the American Economic Association in Atlanta, in 1979, she and other "liberal economists" were unhappy about holding a convention in a state that had not yet ratified the E.R.A. To make up for this, she decided to put in time canvassing for the amendment. — The following, we maintain, is a brief classic.

> I went with two colleagues to take on the shift workers at a small textile plant on the outskirts of the city. Early Friday morning a cab dropped us off in front of the factory. It was a raw December day with

freezing drizzle spitting out of an overcast sky. We huddled together, our fashionable winter coats and high-heeled boots seeming both inadequate and incongruous in this bleak landscape.

At last a siren wailed and a few minutes later workers from the night shift came straggling through the factory gates in twos and threes. I stepped briskly forward holding out my leaflets and reciting my set piece. "Please read about the ERA; it will improve conditions of life for all American women."

The first group of women eyed me suspiciously, then pushed past — roughly. I retreated surprised and intimidated. I was shocked by the appearance of these women: the bulky starch-fed bodies, the careworn faces and bloodshot, exhausted eyes reminded me of the adults who peopled my childhood in South Wales. The minds of these women were clearly on things other than the ERA.

"Can you take little Chrissy today? Ma is laid up; it's her back again, and I've gotta take her in to the clinic," said one to another as she struggled into her plastic raincoat. Her friend sighed. "I guess I can, but drop her off with some milk and food; my old man's drinking again and we don't have much stuff..." Her voice trailed off. These women might have finished work at the factory, but they were about to start another job — dealing with the demands of needy families.

Eventually I engaged the attention of a black woman. Younger than most of the other workers, she accepted some pro-ERA literature and then looked at me antagonistically.

"You know, I've heard of you 'libbers' and your ERA. I've seen that Schlafly person on TV and she says that equal rights for women is a bad deal because we would lose a whole lot. Like us girls get an extra break in the shift, and management can't force us to work overtime the way they force the men."

As she warmed to her theme, her voice rose. "You should try working in this lousy factory week in and week out and I bet you would want all the benefits you could get."

I attempted a comeback. "You know the ERA wouldn't necessarily take job protection away from women; the ones that mean anything would be extended to men. If women need special benefits, so do men."

This factory worker was now really angry. "If you think life's fair, you're crazy," she snapped. "I've got two kids under five and a husband who doesn't lift a finger. What's fair about that? Why shouldn't I get some breaks on the job?" She flung my pamphlets into the gutter and stalked off to the bus stop to wait in the freezing rain for her bus home.

I felt cowed and uncomfortable. It was the last time I canvassed for the ERA.[2]

This account should not be examined for its explicit argumentation. What reached the good professor in her "fashionable winter coat" was the social situation behind the conversation. She had not been told anything she didn't know already — why, she was a professor of *economics!* But what reached her secondhand had, before this, *not* had to be explained to women who worked, who felt on their own backs the meaning of being liberated from "protective" laws.

But let us leave the rest of the Ratification (or Nonratification) Mystery to other books, and return to our muttons: a comment to be made on the mystery that is directly related to the history of the question.

It is simply this: by the late 1970s or thereabouts, the original drive behind the E.R.A. alliance was now gone — disappeared — closed out. The forces that had once kept the E.R.A. alive and pushing now had no more need of it.

This does not refer, of course, to the abstract-doctrinaires of the Alice Paul type, but to the forces that had given political meaning to their abstractions. The deal, we saw, had first been made explicit in the 1920s with the alliance of the N.W.P. with the National Association of Manufacturers. While the women's end was increasingly taken over by the Business and Professional Women's federation, the other end was established by the top leadership of the Republican Party; and this axis was the central alliance for the E.R.A. through the 1950s. The political picture became more complicated with the entrance of the Democratic leadership, but this need not detain us now (it would require an essay on the decline of American liberalism, anyway).

The central alliance had been based on a *quid pro quo:* the symbolic sentence in exchange for the destruction of a few billion dollars' worth of labor laws for workingwomen. That is how the question was posed in (say) the '50s. But as the '70s came to an end, *women's protective laws had already been smashed on a large scale* and bid fair to be wiped out even more completely. Without the passage of an E.R.A.! To be sure, it was the decades-long campaign for "equal rights" that had made possible the semiaccidental phenomenon of Title VII. The National Association of Manufacturers had not wasted its time and energies, and the pro-E.R.A. work of Republican presidents Eisenhower, Nixon, Gerald Ford, et al. had been worth the elocutionary support to Women's Rights.

These campaigns by the E.R.A. alliance had paid off not only in the consequences of Title VII but also in the blows against protective legislation through state instruments, including state E.R.A.'s. But they *had paid off* already; this was in the pluperfect tense. For one of the partners in the alliance, there was no more to be gained by actually placing the E.R.A. in the Constitution now. The ploy had been squeezed dry; the E.R.A. was now a squeezed lemon.

Now it is important to understand that this consideration applies to only one half the mystery. The reasons to which Professor Hewlett points, in her own way, have to do with the revulsion of feeling among American women. Half the alliance did base itself on women's demands, real or fancied. But we are now pointing to the other half of the alliance. *This meant that the hidden drive behind the E.R.A. amendment was no longer there.*

"Hidden" merely means out of sight — not conspiratorial. In a congenial gathering, for example, the oil senator from Texas, John Tower, was perfectly willing to refer to such motivations, in the expectation that his reference would not be a mystery to his audience.

Senator Tower's remarks were made in 1970 before an American Bar Association meeting in St. Louis. He began by noting that the courts could, if they wished, achieve all of the E.R.A.'s objectives through the existing Constitution. This brings us back to the Fourteenth route; indeed Tower thought that "the Fifth and Fourteenth Amendments could easily be construed by the Supreme Court to cover state and federal discrimination on the basis of sex." But the courts have not been of "assistance in solving the discrimination problems in either labor or education." This brought him to the difference between the Fourteenth and a new equal rights amendment:

> Women's work rights have generally not been considered to be covered under the "equal protection" clause [of the Fourteenth]. In *Muller v. Oregon,* a leading 1908 Supreme Court case, the Court upheld a limitation on the number of hours a woman could work in a bakery, declaring that sex was a valid basis of classification.

What this showed was that the Fourteenth route could not, by itself, be relied on to destroy protective legislation.

Unfortunately (Senator Tower pointed out) the E.E.O.C., implementing Title VII, had had a rather poor track record with respect to such laws — at least up to 1970. Title VII did challenge the *Muller v. Oregon* doctrine —

> however, the E.E.O.C. ... has not been very successful to date in winning court cases which it has not initiated in response to specific complaints. Only recently has the Supreme Court agreed to hear a Title VII case.

Hence the Pure E.R.A. was still needed:

> This Amendment *can* serve as a source of momentum for the Supreme Court and the lower courts to actually ... extend the Fifth and Fourteenth Amendments [to cover state and federal sex

discrimination] should they see fit at a date earlier
than the eventual passage and ratification of the Equal
Rights Amendment.

Senator Tower hoped for such a development precisely because
of its removal of "privileges" for women:

It is true that the Equal Rights Amendment may
remove some privileges which women previously
enjoyed... Yet women today seem to be ready to leave
behind the special privileges of the past for full
economic opportunity in the future...[3]

That is, women who were demanding equal access to corporate
Boards of Directors and vice-presidencies were quite willing to "leave
behind the special privileges" enjoyed by the Atlanta textile factory
workers to whom Hewlett talked.

By the mid–1970s the E.E.O.C., implementing Title VII, began
having the desired impact on the target laws. Guidelines were issued
stating that protective labor laws were dis-criminatory; in state after
state, they were destroyed, or mostly so. At the same time that (say)
the Atlanta textile factory workers were getting an inkling of what
was being done to them in the name of equal rights, Senator Tower
was able to look benignly on as the E.E.O.C. did the job it was
supposed to do. Tower did not publicly reverse his position on the
E.R.A., but *in 1978 he fought against the three-year extension of the
ratification deadline.*

Later Tower, in a letter to one of the authors, explained his vote
by saying that seven years was enough for the states' ratification. "To
grant an extension in the emotional aspects of the issue does great
harm to the entire constitutional process."[4] So what was once an

important "source of momentum" was now simply an "emotional issue." What was left after the main goal had been achieved could be dismissed in that way.

If we go back to get the original alliance firmly in mind, if we think back to the rather indecent role of the National Woman's Party in whitewashing the antilabor machinations of the National Association of Manufacturers for the sake of its abstract amendment, then we must realize what has been the crowning irony of the whole history of the E.R.A. That is: these women, who sold themselves to capital for what they thought was suitable compensation, may not even get paid off.

An equal rights amendment of some sort is still a possibility. In these pages, we have seen four different formulas offered for E.R.A.'s that do *not* penalize workingwomen: the early Wisconsin law; the Hayden formulation; the Fourteenth route; and the "Labor E.R.A." that was proposed in California by Anne Draper (see Appendix). There was a fifth if we count Patsy Mink's proposal. It may be that such an E.R.A. may still be usefully taken up.

But if a real women's movement, a workingwomen's movement or one that subsumes workingwomen, arises in this country, it had better first turn its attention away from the Big Abstraction, which in the end means little because it is infinitely manipulable. A movement should have real, concrete "protective" gains to fight for; it is enough to mention Professor Hewlett's emphasis on maternity leave, and also the economic demands that focus on the opprobrious differential in pay (64%) between men and women in this country.

In the end the Pure E.R.A. has been a pure disaster. That is a starting point for moving ahead.

APPENDIX

THE CALIFORNIA EXPERIENCE

Appendix (A) *For a "Labor E.R.A."*

By Anne Draper (January 1972)

[This article was published and widely reprinted in the labor press of California around the beginning of 1972.[1] Anne Draper was the chair of the Union Women's Alliance to Gain Equality (Union W.A.G.E.), as well as a frequent speaker at almost all trade-union conven-tions in the state. It was one of the best summaries of the E.R.A. situation at that point in time.]

The Equal Rights Amendment to the Constitution, as passed by the House a few months ago, is a serious threat to the wages and working conditions of women workers. Unless it is amended in the Senate to include a provision that existing labor standards shall not be destroyed but extended to all workers, men as well as women, the E.R.A. may well destroy the remaining state protective legislation now applicable to women only.

The proposed constitutional amendment would wipe out a host of discriminatory laws against women — laws that should be repealed — such as the prohibition against women bartenders in various state laws. But, unless amended, E.R.A. would have the disastrous effect of also nullifying a large body of truly beneficial legislation covering women workers achieved after decades of struggle. The state of California has the largest body of protective legislation, covering two and a half million women workers and minors.

The state's Industrial Welfare Commission [I.W.C.] was created by legislation passed in 1913 to promote the health, safety and welfare of women and minors. The IWC has issued fourteen industry orders, setting a minimum rate of $1.65 an hour. [Other provisions are summarized here...]

Such provisions, unless extended to men as demanded by women unionists, are in jeopardy because of alleged conflict with Title VII of the federal Civil Rights Act of 1964. The Act prohibits discrimination because of sex, and it has been used in some 17 [later 20–21] states already to strike down all or substantial parts of women's protective legislation.

The E.E.O.C. administering the Act joined in the assault on the trade-union movement and workers generally by chopping down as "discriminatory" any regulation of the hours a woman may work or the weight she may lift. They did not propose reasonable regulation of hours and weights for both men and women workers, which would have ended any discriminatory use of such regulations. Their interpretive guidelines did not say: *Extend protective legislation to men* — an approach which would have protected the benefits and gains made by woman workers.

Earlier this year, the U.S. Court of Appeals ruled, in a case filed by Mrs. Leah Rosenfeld against the Southern Pacific Company, that the state laws limiting the number of hours a woman may work and the weight limit (fifty pounds) were invalid. The state's Division of Industrial Welfare prevailed on the judge not to declare all of California's laws regulating the employment of women invalid, but we are clearly living on borrowed time.

The Rosenfeld decision stands as a terrible warning of what may happen to the minimum wages and working conditions of millions of women workers and minors in this state — the most discriminated against, most depressed, and weakest sector of the working class. Loss of protective laws would be a heavy blow against most of these women workers. It would open the door to cuts in wages and a return to sweatshop conditions, such as we see today in the sweatshops of Chinatown or in the blue-sky sweatshops of California's largest industry, agribusiness.

Only one woman out of five is unionized in this state — a higher average than the national average. Union women could fall back on the protection of a union contract on wages, hours, and other conditions of work. But over 80 percent of the women workers, clustered in low-paying jobs, would face inhuman exploitation and substandard conditions. The federal minimum wage is $1.60 an hour, against the state's $1.65, and for those employed in intrastate work there would be no minimum wage. For farm women, with only partial federal coverage of $1.30 an hour, they could face a 35-cent hourly cut in wages, and more.

The bitter struggle to include farm women and minors under an IWC order took seven years, and it required several more years to obtain the same minimum pay for them as for other women workers, inadequate as it is. What has N.O.W. to say to 100,000 farm women who will suffer a cut in pay and working conditions because N.O.W. insists on what it calls a "pure" amendment?

N.O.W. leaders boast about their "victories" in destroying protective legislation. But such victories are paid for by the blood and sweat of working women. Professional, business and career women don't toil in the fields and orchards of California when temperatures rise over 100 degrees. But for farm women drinking water, washing facilities, and sanitary facilities are vital. Too often the laws are not enforced, but the solution is enforcement, not elimination.

The last few years have witnessed the steady erosion of beneficial state legislation; labor standards for women have been wiped out rather than extended to men workers. Two years ago, and again in the current state legislative session, bills to extend the Industrial Welfare coverage to men have been defeated. Men workers are more highly unionized than women workers, but there are millions of unorganized workingmen partially benefitting by the fallout from women's protective legislation. Should the "pure" E.R.A. pass, the door would be open to equal exploitation — in a depressed economy with rising unemployment.

Employers and corporate interests are in an unholy alliance with business and professional women; the former want to destroy protective legislation since it is costly; the latter are indifferent, if not hostile, to the needs of women workers. N.O.W. is in the contradictory position of saying that they support extending protective legislation to men on a state-by-state basis, while they oppose any amendment to their version of the E.R.A. to guarantee the extension of such legislation to men on a federal level.

Working women want equal rights, equal pay, and equal opportunities, but they do not want to give up any benefit or gain they struggled to win. Extending these benefits and gains to men — and opening up campaigns to improve them — on a state and federal level would unite men and women workers on the basis of equal rights for all.

(Appendix B)
The California Campaign for a "Labor E.R.A."

By Hal Draper (1976)

[After Anne Draper's death in March 1973, material was prepared for a memorial publication. The following was written as a story of the work that she had done in this field as chair of Union W.A.G.E. But it is, I think, a useful account of a situation which has now gone down the Memory Hole, along with the rest of the Hidden History, namely, the *transitional* situation when a fight against the worst consequences of the E.R.A. ploy could still be made. Very incidentally, it is also a record of my own education on this issue. — H.D.]

During the period when the states' ratification of the E.R.A. was still hanging fire, there was a last effort made by workingwomen to salvage women's labor laws from the destructive impact of Congress' action, now superadded to the previous impact of Title VII. This effort was most significant in California.

1. *Labor in California*
There were two reasons why a special part of the drama was acted out in California, particularly during 1970–1972.

(a) California, with the largest body of women workers (10 percent of the 31 million nationally) also had the most substantial body of protective legislation for women workers left in the country. There was still a big stake.

(b) The effort was sparked by an independent movement of trade-union women, the Union Women's Alliance to Gain Equality (Union W.A.G.E.). It had been organized by Anne Draper; and while it made some progress in gaining adherents and correspondents in other states, it was seriously active only in California. Based on the San Francisco Bay Area, it had important associates in the Los Angeles area too. This group was the catalyst which moved bigger forces into motion, including (at times) the state labor apparatus as well as individual unions.

The California legislation *not* yet destroyed may serve as an example of what women workers had lost elsewhere:

○ Minimum wage of $1.65 an hour; overtime pay after eight hours a day or 40 hours a week.

○ Other working-time provisions, such as: lunch breaks of not less than 30 minutes in five hours; rest periods of 10 minutes every four hours.

○ Other money provisions, dealing with: employer-supplied uniforms and protective garments, when required; report-in pay; split-shift pay; cost of tools; meal and room charges; no tip deduction; cash shortage and breakage; etc.

○ Working conditions concerning: decent standards of cleanliness, lighting, ventilation, temperature, drinking water, toilets, available rest rooms, locker rooms and dressing rooms, seats on the job, first aid, elevator service, second exits —

○ And other provisions, making up about fifty specifics to protect "health, welfare and safety."

These gains, and similar lists of on-job benefits for women workers which had been acquired and consolidated in painful struggles over most of a century, are certain to bore the business, professional and career women who boast about "the victories we have won in removing protective legislation." This quotation was from the pen of Aileen Hernandez,[2] N.O.W. leader and sometime president, who liked to tell critics she was once educational director for a trade union, and who, *much* more recently, had been celebrated in the San Francisco press as one of the highly paid businesswoman-successes in the area. Her winged words played a bit of a role in Union W.A.G.E.'s campaign.

But these gains look different to (say) the women of the farm workers, who have to labor in the fields without available toilets or drinking water as long as such legislation does not exist for them — or even when it does exist, unless the union can enforce the regulations.

On the other hand, women professors and upwardly mobile businesswomen, fighting for justifiable upgrading in defiance of prejudice, do not usually have to worry about lunch breaks, let alone fight for them. They can afford to think that protective legislation is "insulting." Some 100,000 women workers of the needle trades in the Los Angeles area alone, largely black and Mexican-American, depend on these hard-won gains for a partial measure of humanization of work.

Even so, little would have happened without the initiatives and intervention of Union W.A.G.E. The California Labor Federation (the state organization), like the national AFL-CIO, would hardly have moved energetically on this issue without prodding. A word on the role of the labor movement is necessary for the background.

The propaganda of N.O.W. and similar feminists, far removed from the life of working women, systematically seeks to represent the trade-union movement *en bloc* as simply a plot of male chauvinists. In general, the image of trade-unionism which is regularly assumed in *Ms* magazine, as in N.O.W., is the same as that presented in press editorials about Big Labor, or in sociology classes (where many of these women learned it), or in TV cops-and-robbers serials about corrupt union gangsters. What these people do not understand about the labor movement is its most vital characteristic: it is a house with many mansions, in which all kinds of things happen, apart from what happens at the tops.

All of the worst characteristics of the trade-union movement exist because the unions are *embedded* in a society where those characteristics are dominant. The top apparatus structures and many unions are, of course, male-dominated and male-chauvinist in tendency: almost all the dominant structures of American society are. And this is exactly why trade-union women have to organize autonomously within the union world; so thought the founders of Union W.A.G.E.

The leaders of the American labor movement are good Americans; that is, they are good and American — being representative of this society. If it is charged that the unions often fail to protect the interests of women workers, the question that has to be answered is this: does the critic understand that the same AFL-CIO protects the interests of *men* workers only spottily, and that the trade-union tool works for workers only insofar as they take it in hand themselves?

The women who founded Union W.A.G.E. organized from below, and did not expect the state union officials to fight their battles for them. But they exerted themselves to put pressure on these and all officials to fight battles, on the right side. And they did so.

One of the N.O.W. myths is that the AFL-CIO for many years opposed the Pure E.R.A. because of male domination. This is contrary-to-truth. For several decades, it was the Women's Trade Union League and other women's organizations sympathetic to labor — but completely independent of and even hostile to the A.F.L. — that spearheaded the fight against the Pure amendment, while the labor federation passed resolutions and did lobbying.*

In the 1960s, with social-feminism moribund and with the shift to the "New Feminism," the unions — just as male-dominated as before — came over to the Pure line. Some of the internationals (i.e., national unions) came out for the Pure E.R.A. under various pressures, in particular the pressure of their political alliance with the Democrats. Some interesting things happened...

> ○ The American Federation of Teachers did so among the first. After all, women teachers (unionist or not) often resemble the career women that dominate N.O.W. more than they do the sweated seamstresses of the needle trades. But at the 1972 convention of the A.F.T., a ginger group of women teachers educated and inspired by Union W.A.G.E., made their case clear. *And as a result the A.F.T. reversed its position,* to support the Union W.A.G.E. demand for a "Labor E.R.A."

---

* This has been covered in some chapters of the present book. We may add, in hindsight, that the AFL-CIO leadership began to shift its formal position on the amendment in accordance with the line of the Democratic Party. By the time the Democrat Birch Bayh became the E.R.A.'s floor manager, the AFL-CIO had been brought into line. — H.D.

○ A similar thing happened with the Communications Workers of America, which has a very large female membership. The male-dominated leadership had come out *for* the Pure E.R.A. It was only when a group of rank-and-file women unionists, again helped by Union W.A.G.E., brought the issue sharply before a national convention of the union, and explained what was at stake, that the union adopted a new position.

○ Of course, the Teamsters Union — the leading union that supported Richard Nixon for president — continued to support the Pure E.R.A. Mythologists will have to explain some day how it was that the purest of pure Male-Chauvinist Pigs became the leaders of Pure feminism, in the footsteps of George Wallace...

The showcase union for the Pure E.R.A. advocates was the United Auto Workers. The reasons have more to do with a different question, viz., what has happened to the American labor movement as its percentage of unionization steadily decreased to 19 percent. The U.A.W., once justly regarded as one of the more progressive unions in the country, is today not a shadow of its former self; its apparatus is increasingly indistinguishable from any other organization of porkchoppers in the great American tradition of Get-Yours-for-No.1. But aside from this development, there is another and very illuminating consideration.

It is this: the women workers in the Auto Union are in one of the most thoroughly unionized industries in the country. To a much greater extent than the mass of workers, *they* do not need protective laws, since it is the union that provides for their protection in practice. (This is what led the old A.F.L. of the 1920s to oppose labor legislation for *men,* in its shortsighted way.) In supporting the Pure amendment which will destroy labor legislation for heavily exploited women workers in fields or factories, these U.A.W. women leaders are saying in effect: The destruction of your protective legislation is no skin off *our* lasses. They can get by, because the union is their protective shield. This is the old (and ever new) unionism of special interest, with one trade knifing another to get some real or fancied advantage, with the skilled trades knifing the unskilled, *ad infinitum, ad nauseam* — just as happily as the great American spirit in which one businessman knifes another in the name of free enterprise.

It was Union W.A.G.E. that revived the labor wing of social-feminism. It was *not* established as a women's committee of the union structure, hence inhibited by all the institutional hangups of the latter. It was *not* a group of outsiders assuming to speak in the name of workingwomen (as even the old Women's Trade Union League had been in part). It was built around a core of women workers who operated as good trade-unionists, acting inside the labor movement or outside as necessary, and at the same time it was organizationally independent.

It happened that the then head of the California Federation of Labor was John Henning, who considered himself a sort of closet social-democrat (at least in that period). This did not mean that he was ready to rush into radical enterprises, but he was susceptible to reasonable pressure, especially for good causes. It is a fact that Union W.A.G.E. did move the state AFL-CIO under Henning into significant support of its campaigns; but there was no control either way. The simplistic view of labor — Evil Male Chauvinists vs. Champions of Equal Rights — was never farther from the truth than it was during this period. "Labor" was not monolithic.

2. *The Campaign for "Extension"*

The Union Women (as we may call the Union W.A.G.E. people for short) exerted their greatest efforts around this campaign, along the lines explained in Anne Draper's article, which had received good circulation in the state trade-union movement. Its aim was an equal rights amendment which would preserve women workers' gains *by extending them to men.*

The "Extension" idea had been around for a long time, and was not new. N.O.W. propagandists commonly gave the idea lip service by assuring hearers that such extension was what *would* happen when the E.R.A. was adopted (or "would probably happen," if they felt like making a concession to honesty). All that the Union Women's campaign said was: *Let's get that put on the books in black and white.*

Against this simple idea the standard arguments of the Pure had little or nothing to say to women workers. When N.O.W. advocates or Pure E.R.A. champions had to confront this Extension campaign in California, they offered a grab bag of arguments that were not always responsive.

(a) They often simply denounced protective legislation *per se* as a male-chauvinist plot against women's rights, following the same script that they might have used in any other state. But in confrontation with the Union Women's campaign for Extension, it ceased to make sense. If you're ready to reassure worried women that the E.R.A. *did* mean extension — or that you wanted it to — then why not get it written down?

(b) They often claimed that protective legislation was no longer a problem because Title VII had wiped it all out anyway, or was going to. But this was quite false as a matter of fact, especially in California — as we have seen. Title VII had wrought havoc, to be sure, and we have described what it did; but in (say) 1972 the Pure E.R.A. advocates were overanticipating the range of destruction. *Were* they interested in preserving what was possible — through Extension? A single debate was enough to show the Union Women that they were not very much interested...

© Other Pure speakers might argue, on the contrary, that the E.R.A. was needed precisely because Title VII was too limited, or because the E.R.A. would do in one swoop what Title VII might do only after long court battles. But on examination, in the light of the Union Women's proposal, this could only mean they were in a hurry to wipe out protective laws *before* Extension could get to work.

(d) Back to the reassurances: they could claim — and did sporadically claim — that the E.R.A.'s one-sentence blast *would* be interpreted by the courts to require the extension of protective legislation (or some of it) to men. This brash claim hung by two threads.

> (1) One thread was the assurance of some pro-E.R.A. lawyer that this court interpretation would (or could, or might, or should) take place. These happy assurances were still being ladled into N.O.W. press statements even after twenty states had totally or partially cut back protective legislation, *without* extension to men, on the basis of Title VII.

> (2) The second thread was a single case in a single state in 1970: in Arkansas a federal court had extended a benefit (time-and-a-half for overtime) to men, the so-called Potlatch Forest case. In the Pure

E.R.A.'s propaganda, the Potlatch Forest case became for a little while the sum-total of American jurisprudence, and Arkansas was more important than the Supreme Court.

The claim itself was always either phantasmagoria or demagogy, usually the former. The latter possibility received institutional support from the E.E.O.C. in April 1972, when it issued new "Guidelines" purporting to further the Extension pattern. For a while N.O.W. announced that the whole issue was now solved, everyone could support the Pure E.R.A. with an easy heart. When Anne Draper unearthed the actual text of the Guidelines (with interesting difficulty), the reality turned out to be quite different. Mostly the heralded extension was simply left up to the individual employer: if "employers can prove [to whom?] that business necessity prohibits extending them [the benefits]," then they "shall not provide such benefit to members of either sex." *Employers were here being instructed on the grounds for dropping such benefits for women as well as men.* (We all know about "business necessity.")

There was a slight difference in the treatment of wage and overtime provisions, but the sentiments expressed in the Guidelines were neither laws nor enforceable regulations, and bound nobody. They were supposed to "guide" attorneys general and courts, but no one ever found an attorney general or a court that extended benefits because of the Guidelines. On the other hand, the instruction that "the employer shall not provide these benefits" was automatically enforced with ironclad efficiency — by the employers.

It was a typical Washingtonian bureaucratic fraud, its only point being to dislocate the fight for Extension, which was threatening to become a popular watchword in some quarters.

3. *Another View of the Debate*

Let us turn to another account of the California debate on this issue. It was provided by an article, published in *Society* in 1974 by Miller and Linker,[3] which gave a fairly evenhanded summary. The authors explained four arguments which the E.R.A. proponents used to counteract the concern about protective legislation. These are summarized below; and to these we append comments reflecting the replies given by the Union Women.

(1) *Some of the protective laws are beneficial to women, to be sure, but some do represent restrictions on women.*

This statement was true, and the truth had been noted in Anne Draper's "For a Labor E.R.A." What remained unexplained by the E.R.A. proponents was why this reasonable statement justified a one-blast E.R.A. whose sole virtue was that it aimed to indiscriminately destroy *every* sex-differentiated law, including every possible beneficial one. The Union Women argued: Let's keep the good ones, and knock out the bad ones only.

In short, if the argument was that there were "some" over restrictive laws, the one kind of solution that was not indicated was a one-blast destroy-it-all E.R.A.

(2) *E.R.A. proponents "pointed to the injustices created by this so-called protection and relied on examples used by Martha Griffiths, chief sponsor of the amendment, in the U.S. Congressional debates."*

Representative Griffiths' much-used examples illuminated the issue, but not in her light. One of her favorites was this: it is hypocritical, she charged, to protect certain women workers against (say) night-work hazards, but to leave charwomen and women entertainers uncovered by these laws. Hypocrisy, yes — but whose?

Charwomen *should* be covered by the protective laws, and the Union Women would not only advocate this but also go out and organize them. It was Griffiths' pro-E.R.A. majority, with much help from the others, who for decades had kept charwomen and the like in their place — the same Congressional majority that kept voting down Equal Pay bills. It was not Griffiths' organization, the Business and Professional Women's federation, that ever fought to cover the disadvantaged and poor with labor legislation. So — *whose* hypocrisy was Griffiths showing up?

Anyway, how was Griffiths' example an argument for her E.R.A.? The implicit argument was this: since charwomen can still be over exploited by employers, then the women of the needle-trades workers and farm workers and others might as well be sweated too...

As for entertainers: the Union Women agreed that they need not be automatically covered by the same laws as the mass of wage-workers, precisely because their conditions were often so different. Indeed, Griffiths never actually proposed that existing protective laws should all necessarily cover entertainers. But it was she, not the Union Women, who proposed a law that had to fit indiscriminately everybody in sight.

The Union Women agreed that some protective laws had an important fault, in intruding too much into the province of career women, whose conditions and needs might be different from charwomen and farm workers. They said: Let us remedy these errors by amending the protective laws, not by destroying them.

The inconsistency was Griffiths', but it was not a matter of hypocrisy. It was a question of a mentality, a style of thinking. When she seemed to say in effect, "If you restrict night work by some women, you must restrict it for every female in the country," this ultimatistic view reflected her typical career-woman type of sexism: "women" constitute a monolithic group, to be treated monolithically. It is the other side of a coin whose flip side shows us the well-known MCP who likes global aphorisms like "Women are illogical..."

(3) *Suits have been brought against protective laws by blue-collar women. "The involvement of blue-collar women in the campaign for [E.R.A.] ratification was also stressed in order to negate the charge that the E.R.A. was solely a middle-class phenomenon."*

This was a debaters' point which could appeal only to the "middle-class phenomenon" — feminists who think of workingwom-en as a beast with one neck; the monolithic view again. A moment's thought about the tens of millions of "blue-collar" workers in this country should be enough. The sponsors of the antilabor "Right to Work" laws, notoriously used to smash trade-unionism, would have no trouble digging up a few blue-collar workers (Certified Proletarians) to testify for them. George Wallace had black supporters. There were German Jews who supported Hitler. Jay Gould used to boast that he could hire one-half the working class to kill the other half; and while this is a polemical exaggeration, it points to a well-known problem — which has nothing to do with the E.R.A.

(4) *"They stressed that no constitutional amendment has ever operated to automatically nullify any law."*

In this connection, the semiliberal lobbying group called Common Cause was cited as pointing to the Arkansas Potlatch precedent. The inflation of this Arkansas case has been discussed. But another word is necessary about the generalization itself.

To say that a constitutional amendment does not "automatically" nullify any law is either a platitude or an irrelevancy. It is a platitude if it is merely saying that a court decision has to be rendered first. It is an irrelevancy if the problem is not any automatism but a realistic appraisal of the impact of a given measure after considerable experience. But Common Cause does not favor a law-by-law appraisal. It is one of the loudest of E.R.A. proponents in insisting (in other sections of its argumentation) that every sex-differentiated law must be destroyed by court decree as soon as the E.R.A. is on the books.

4. *The Argument from Technology*

Another frequent argument against protective legislation was based on the state of technology. It permits a valuable insight into the thinking of the E.R.A. proponents. It was very common in the literature, but we can give it here from an official source: the above-mentioned E.E.O.C. Guidelines of April 1972:

> The Commission believes that such State laws and regulations, although originally promulgated for the purpose of protecting females, have ceased to be relevant to our technology or to the expanding role of the female worker in our economy. The Commission has found that such laws and regulations do not take into account the capacities, preferences, and abilities of individual females and tend to discriminate rather than protect.

Why are protective laws not "relevant to our technology"? The argument was repeated endlessly, rarely explained, and when clarified, largely based on one kind of protective law: weightlifting restrictions. The "argument from technology" sounded much more impressive when it was not explained.

For the large majority of protective laws, the argument from technology immediately points in favor, not against. The possibility of providing toilets in the fields for farm workers was created by modern technology; it was impracticable for thirteenth-century peasants. A good many of the working conditions that protective laws call for — like elevators in multistory buildings — would be unthinkable without modern technology. But let us ignore this fact, and confront the "argument from technology" on the single side-arena where it has some limited point.

The argument is that our technology presumably makes heavy weight-lifting by women workers so close to obsolete that the problem can be ignored. If this were so, then the weight-lifting *restrictions* could also be ignored, and would be no problem. If no one is lifting heavy weights, then the restrictive laws are simply gathering dust. If they are so important that the E.R.A. proponents like to talk about them more than about toilets in the field, there must be something wrong with the original argument.

The people who wrote this sort of E.R.A. propaganda really thought that machinery did all the heavy lifting in American industry. Someone told them so, and it sounded reasonable to people behind a desk. It suggests that these people literally cannot grasp what industrial work is like. Like Griffiths' much-repeated conundrum about the charwomen and the entertainers, another brushoff common in E.R.A. propaganda was the following bit: *Do those male chauvinists who want to restrict women's weight-lifting in industry worry about weight-lifting by a housewife who has to carry her baby up and down stairs during a day?* It was widely pointed out that babies often weigh more than fifty pounds, the protective-law limit in California.

Let us look at industrial weight-lifting, not in the abstract but with the help of a couple of vignettes that figured in the Union Women's campaign.

(a) In the early 1970s, women members of an independent union, the Association of Pulp and Paper Workers did pioneer work with an interesting form of organization they had devised themselves, called "Women, Inc." Its president, Hazle Perry Hill of Antioch, California, was a worker at Crown Zellerbach of 23 years standing. In the union she was not only a vice-president but editor of its paper (though the union as a whole was male-dominated as usual). She was also a mother with four children, and had to earn a living by working. The women workers in this industry had fought for equal pay, and had won this demand in 1968. They had had a significant part in the fight to get the provision "sex" added to the state Fair Employment Practices act.

When Hazle Perry Hill discovered Union W.A.G.E., she applied for membership, and in her letter incidentally mentioned that she had a problem:

> Right now, I'm attempting to do a job that has a history of being male. It is hard physical labor, and after two weeks, I wonder if I'll ever make it! The spirit is willing, the flesh is weak. I must push 2000 lb. rolls of paper about ten times a day.
>
> I must climb a ladder and rethread this huge machine several times a shift. I think I'm trying so hard to

prove that a woman can do this that I might fail. I've never been so tired and hurt in so many places as I do now. I want to give it back but I'm too damned stubborn and determined to succeed to prove a point. Wish me luck — I need it.

Right now, we have no state laws — they were pitched out over a year ago. Some of them, you must admit, need to be revised.

Crown Zellerbach is a giant corporation, not a fly-by-night operation, and presumably understands the state of technology. Aren't there machines that can push tons of paper around? There are. They represent huge capital investments. Why spend this money if you can hire workers to do the pushing at a fraction of the investment cost? (This, of course, applies to men as to women.) We see immediately that the argument from the level of technology has little to do, necessarily, with how that technology is used to produce a maximum profit. And the smaller the company, the less likely is it to make maximum use of available technology where another solution is immediately more profitable, given a certain level of wages. Economists will tell us that overexploitation of labor is a factor that *inhibits* the full exploitation of technology; and the spread of labor legislation is a factor that compels the economic system toward maximum modernization — however reluctantly.

If the protective law limiting weight-lifting for women were extended to men, in line with the Extension Campaign of the Union Women, corporations would be thereby induced to make use of available technology, or at any rate be pushed in that direction. Some day the fantasy in the minds of the E.R.A. proponents might even become a reality, in spite of them.

But back to the case of Hazle Perry Hill. She was not really typical — first, because she apparently *could* have changed her job if she had wanted to (though there may have been penalties not stated in her letter); and second, we have here an extra-ordinary woman with a powerful feminist motivation.

(b) The norm was better exemplified by a letter which was reprinted around this time by the paper of the Western Pulp and Paper Workers (reported also by *Union W.A.G.E.,* the group's paper). This letter was written by a rank-and-file member in the Camas (Washington) local of the union, Mary Mabry. It was written in a spirit of bitterness which will no doubt appall all N.O.W. types who have to carry babies up and down stairs:

> I wish to take this opportunity to thank all of you women's liberation members for what you have done for the women employees of Crown Zellerbach of Camas.
>
> Women were once protected by state law as to how much they could lift, how many hours they could work, and certain machinery and tools they were not to use for safety reasons.
>
> Now that you "wonderful" women have helped liberate us, we are suddenly able to push 1,000-pound carts, lift heavy paper, bags and bales and work 12-hour shifts with nothing but a 15-minute lunch break.
>
> A 61-year-old widow who has worked for years in the bag factory hurt her back on the job. She went to

tell "the men upstairs" that she could not do that heavy lifting. They told her if she couldn't do her job she could quit. She has only one year to retirement and has been a good, faithful worker, yet they couldn't care less!

Many of us women have complained about the heavy work we are now required to do. The "men upstairs" tell us that we are getting equal pay for men, so we are to work like men. Many women have had to quit. Right now, I am in the hospital in traction because of the heavy lifting I am required to do.

If any of you women's lib suckers (or other interested parties) want to take a real look at what you've done for us, come visit "the snake pit" at Camas and try some of the jobs — if you think you are man enough.[4]

What have we to say to Mary Mabry and to the host of women workers in her position? We can, of course, denounce her as a sexist (unless we assume that "man enough" is satirical), and prescribe a consciousness-raising session with the local housewives — that is, as soon as she gets out of the hospital. If she had to quit her job at management's suggestion, she would have plenty of time for this activity. Reading the literature on the E.R.A., she would learn that she should not let a little thing like a wrenched back interfere with "the expanding role of the female worker in our economy" (at 64 percent of men's wages), and certainly not interfere with other women who want to make it up there with "the men upstairs."

We have previously compared the Pure E.R.A. mentality with the "Right to Work" mentality. Translated into abstract-feminist terms, it says: *If we do the same work as men, we ought to get equal pay; and, turn-about, if we get equal pay, then we must not object to working under the same (inferior) conditions as men.* But the second proposition does not follow from the first. If the two propositions seem intertwined in abstract logic, it is only because they are taken as static descriptions of a world we cannot do anything about. But the history of the labor movement and its struggles is a history of proving that this academic logic is empty. Where trade-union organization is strong enough, this or that sector of workers continually wins special conditions that begin by being "unfair" to others — as the employers will be the first to proclaim in the name of supernal Justice. All these outcries mean is that one sector of labor has forged ahead for the nonce.

Modern technology, or rather its present-day utilization, has not abolished weight-lifting by either men or women. With the destruction of protective laws, excessive weight-lifting then becomes obligatory for women workers, as the "equal rights" device is used by management to maximize profits, in some cases by pressing women to quit employment. When the state E.R.A. or Title VII destroys protective legislation, a certain vacuum is left, and this vacuum is inevitably filled by the ever-present autocratic power of management over the worker. In its simplest terms, the famous victory won by the destruction of protective laws meant that Crown Zellerbach was itself the administrator of "equal rights" for women and men workers.

We have agreed that, while modern technology has not abolished weight-lifting, it does make it possible to limit excessive weight-lifting, by both men and women, to special categories. This points to the modernization (revision) of protective legislation in given cases, after concrete reappraisals of its operation. Hazle Perry

Hill's letter had made this point, without knowing the stand taken by the Union Women. It was, in fact, the viewpoint of the Union Women.

In a debate on the E.R.A. with the local N.O.W. president,[5] Anne Draper, on behalf of Union W.A.G.E., had put it this way:

> ... In May 1971 the court in California nullified, abolished, any limits on the pounds that a woman worker could lift or the hours she could work. I consider this an equality of exploitation. For example, a woman farm worker can now be told: *Take this lug of tomatoes, which weighs 50 to 70 Pounds, and run with it — not walk, but RUN with it to the truck five times an hour.* We now have equality — no limits on hours or wages. Let me tell you what our position was. We felt that no workers should be treated in the dehumanizing and vicious way that a lot of industry treats them. We are not beasts of burden. If we can figure out how to get a machine to move with 9000 parts that work beautifully, then we ought to be able to figure out machines that do the weight-lifting for both men and women on the job. We asked for reasonable limitations of hours for both men and women. We don't want to see women fighting for a return to the ten- or twelve-hour day. We want to see a five- or six-hour day.

By the time of this debate, the bottom-line issue in California was concretized in a way somewhat more dramatic than in other states.

5. *Bottom Line: Extend or Destroy?*

By 1970 the dispute in California had heated up, as a number of big corporations sought to use Title VII to do what they had been trying to do for decades — namely, save some millions (perhaps billions) of dollars by getting rid of the whole body of women's labor legislation. At a legislative hearing in February, representatives of six employers' associations called impatiently for the suspension of all state protective laws that were in litigation. The National Right to Work Committee, coordinating group of the hard-line union-busting elements, stepped up its activity in California as well as in some other key states.

The Fibreboard Corporation in the Antioch–Stockton area took the lead in the drive to return women workers' conditions to the nineteenth century, in the name of equal rights and Title VII. Around the turn of the year, it announced (on its own say-so) that federal law had voided all state protective laws, and it set January 15, 1970 as the deadline for changing its working conditions in accordance, regardless of California health and safety laws. Women were now going to be forced to work 12 to 16 hours straight, instead of the more expensive three-shift system; they would have to lift as much as 150 pounds a minute; rest periods and lunch hours were cut to pieces. Women workers were played against each other, by allowing some departments lunch breaks and others none. One woman reported that in her plant the workers were allowed three ten-minute breaks in an eight-hour period, with no lunch break, and were forbidden to eat while working.

(On the wall was a notice informing the happy workers that the Civil Rights Act of 1964 prohibited sex discrimination and called for equality on the job. Rejoice! Management was going to enforce "equality" to the last broken back.)

Another well-known champion of human rights, the state Telephone Company, joined the rampant forces of equality with a memo to managers to ignore certain labor provisions which a district court had knocked out with Title VII. Ma Bell started changing shift hours with abandon; for example, one woman's new schedule put her to work from nine at night to three in the morning, with her second shift starting at six the *same* morning.

This vanguard of "Everything goes" equality was followed by smaller imitators. A Los Angeles company that farmed out household workers abolished payment of overtime to women working twelve-hour stints, and told a federal court: Title VII "abolished chivalry, at least as far as employment practices are concerned." The court agreed that chivalry was detestable.

The whole body of women's labor laws, all that was left of it, was hanging by a thread in the courts, as the court machinery creaked under the pressures to invalidate *everything* by judicial decree on the basis of Title VII. The juridical front of this drive was taken over by the pro-E.R.A. feminists, who launched a new campaign to administer the *coup de grâce.* The *coup,* without much *grâce,* was to get a state E.R.A. on the books, since the national E.R.A. might take years to ratify.

It may seem that the proposal for a state E.R.A. was routine; but *at this point* there was more to it than met the eye. The Union Women were in course of mobilizing support for legislation to extend the protective laws to men. The prospects for this Extension campaign were good; support was being gathered steadily especially through the state trade-union movement. There was a real possibility; or — viewed from the opposite side — there was a real danger...

At this point, the issue was posed on a knife edge: if a state E.R.A. were adopted *before* the Extension was won then there would be nothing to extend, for the sex-discriminatory labor laws would all be simply smashed by the state instrument.

The Union Women concretized the immediate issue by presenting the following proposition to N.O.W. and its people: *Join forces with us NOW to get the Extension legislation through. Then we — and organized labor, we pledge — will work all-out to put the State E.R.A. on the books.*

The key part of this proposition was the following: *Do not insist on pushing the state E.R.A. to a quick vote in Sacramento before Extension can be won.*

Through a chain of circumstances, never had the focal issue of the E.R.A. been posed so sharply as now, at this point. The E.R.A. activists could get a quick state E.R.A. which might benefit some career women, but only over the backs of the farm women workers in the fields, the needle-trades workers in the Los Angeles sweatshops, the women in the paper mills, and a million other "sisters."

N.O.W.'s answer was to drive all-out to get the state E.R.A. adopted as speedily as possible.

They also passed resolutions in favor of Extension. Since their hearts bled for their exploited sisters, they promised — whenever queried — that after all the protective laws had been destroyed, they would pass more resolutions in favor of labor legislation for everyone. But first things first: *First we get ours, then we'll worry about you stepsisters.*

There were many discussions in this period between the Union Women and members of N.O.W. (discussions that played a more important part in my own education than in that of the N.O.W. people, I'm afraid). One of the things that the Union Women tried to explain, not too successfully, was what decades of work it had taken to win the concessions that N.O.W. wanted to destroy with one document. In the above-mentioned formal debate with N.O.W., Anne

Draper tried to make this a little more vivid just with regard to the most recent phase — the adoption of wage orders by the Industrial Welfare Commission (I.W.C.):

> Let me give you a personal note on what it took to achieve these [I.W.C.] wage orders. In 1958–1959, after five years of hearings, concluding hearings were being held simply to determine whether a wage order should be issued covering farm women workers' health, welfare and safety. Five years of hearings!
>
> Arrayed against us were the banks, the insurance companies, and of course the largest industry in the state, agribusiness — a four-billion dollar industry which said it could not afford to pay a $1 an hour minimum wage for farm women. The Industrial Welfare Commission consisted of five people appointed by the governor, and till recently all five came from management, not one represented labor.
>
> After five years of hearings, in which women and children testified to the incredible conditions under which they picked the state's fruits and vegetables, the Commission finally voted to issue an industry order. That, dear friends, took another two years of hearings. People like Dolores Huerta and César Chavez and other farm worker leaders mobilized the support of men, women, and children working in the fields, plus allies from the trade-union movement.

Finally, *finally* we got Order 14 — a miserable one, inferior; they wouldn't even give the same wage to farm women as to other women workers. Nevertheless, it established the right of the farm woman worker to have drinking water available in the fields (or at least the right to sue in court for it). And it established her right to have a toilet available in the field. It has been easier to get a toilet on the moon than in the fields of California; but nevertheless the legal right now exists in this state.

Every employer group in California has sought to break down these industry orders. Would it not be ironic if they could use as their façade, their front, a women's group that says it is fighting for equality and equal rights for women?

No use. In this debate the N.O.W. speaker* concluded her argument with the following words, which deserve to be preserved, as a high-water mark of utter confusion:

Protective legislation is not the problem. We're all working to extend protective legislation. I cannot understand why we have to have it tied to the Equal Rights Amendment, which covers a much broader area, which covers women who really don't give a damn about protective legislation because they're not working. Why sacrifice the rest of your life? You

---

* An interesting sidelight: the speaker was Diane Watson, then president of San Francisco N.O.W. As it happened, she was employed as the personnel director of a restaurant chain — which had been recently involved in breaking a union organizing drive. But she was a victim, too: not long afterward, she was fired from her job — for devoting too much time to N.O.W. affairs. A parable for the textbooks.

know, protective legislation is a bone, as it were, thrown to women. We're protected for eight hours a day and the rest of our lives we can go hang. Now, I don't think that we have to risk the rest of our lives for eight hours a day. Especially since it's very simple to keep protective legislation by extending it through a majority vote. It simply does not make sense. I don't see what this debate is about and I cannot understand the question. Thank you.

This parting word was sincere, at any rate. It is the voice of one living in another world than that of workingwomen concerned about toilets in the field. Twice it says "I cannot understand," and it is up to us to understand this incapacity to understand.

The N.O.W. organization in Sacramento, the state capital, gave a different response to the Extension campaign, equally sincere. It wrote in its newsletter: "Not all lawmakers who have cosponsored the state E.R.A. are in support of extending protective laws to men."[6] Exactly so. The bloc that was going to put a state E.R.A. on the books depended on the votes of the same creatures of the growers who had voted for decades to keep the farm workers under. (The history of the national E.R.A. should make this pattern clear.)

The political realism of N.O.W. was exemplary, and could not be faulted as an expression of American politics. It could be briefly and bluntly summarized in the following way: *We aim to get our E.R.A. by making a deal with the state's sweatshoppers, union-busters and corporate profiteers. Not that we like them, but there's no other way. It's a matter of making a fair exchange: they, the big economic interests, will be happy because (for example) the growers will no longer be harassed by unreasonable demands like toilets in the fields; and WE will be happy because (say) women professors in the big knowledge factories will find it easier to get ahead. Then after this quid pro quo, we will be in a position to indulge our sentimentality and sincerely pass resolutions in favor of extending protective legislation to men. Although it will be inconvenient if it no longer exists to be extended. You can't have everything. Just so long as we get ours.*

This policy worked out, in the sense that the California legislature adopted a state E.R.A. in 1972.

For a symbol: the first thing that happened next was that the Bank of America announced that it would discontinue the special service for women workers on the night shift which provided taxis to take the women home safely. This was now "sex discrimination" and highly illegal — no more legal, indeed, than muggings. Women could take their chances: men did, didn't they?

Other corporations followed suit, even though lawsuits were still pending on the issues involved. Labor forces did manage to get the legislature to pass a bill extending the *powers* of the I.W.C. to men — its powers only, not the existing orders. But the governor, one Ronald Reagan, vetoed the bill, announcing that "all the leading business interests in the state are against this bill." The N.O.W. people, whose hearts still beat as one for exploited sisterhood, rapidly lost interest in the whole matter.

The work of Union W.A.G.E. in mobilizing the labor movement's support in the Extension campaign was not entirely without result. Legislation was gotten through to salvage the extension of the minimum wage to men and to preserve the I.W.C. itself. The contents of the various I.W.C. orders went into a sort of administrative limbo. In the end California could not avoid reflecting the national situation.

Reference Notes

Note: In many cases, the source of a reference is already indicated in the text, as in the case of citations from the *Congressional Record,* where the date of the session is given. — Where the abbreviation *op. cit.* is used, it is followed by a parenthetical reference to the note involved, by chapter and note number; except where the reference is to the note immediately preceding. For example, references to Lemons' book (Chapter 1, note 1) look so: *op. cit.* (1: n.1). — References to a multicolumn work are in colon form; that is, Vol. 4, page 30 = 4:30.

Forward

1. Tasneem Raja, "Gangbang Interviews" and "Bikini Shots": Silicon Valley's Brogrammer Problem, *Mother Jones*, April 26, 2012, (http://www.motherjones.com/media/2012/04/silicon-valley-brogrammer-culture-sexist-sxsw#correction).
2. Sheryl Sandberg, *Lean In: Women, Work and the Will to Lead* (2013).
3. National Organization for Women, *Wai-Mart: The Facts* http://www.now.org/issues/wfw/wm-facts.html).
4. Alexis Kleinman, Marissa Mayer Pokes Fun at Walmart Protestors, *The Huffington Post*, November 20, 2013 (http://huffingtonpost.com/2013/11/20/marissa-mayer-walmart_n_4310069.html
5. *Lean In* at 102.
6. Maureen Dowd, Get Off Your Cloud, *The New York Times*, February 25, 2013. (http://www.nytimes.com/2013/02/27/opinion/dowd-get-off-your-cloud)
7. *Lean In* at 10.
8. Ibid.

Preface

1. An exception: we collaborated to produce a booklet on the connections between the growers and the University of California, *The Dirt on California: Agribusiness and the University,* by Anne Draper and Hal Draper (Berkeley, 1968).
2. Sylvia Ann Hewlett, *A Lesser Life; The Myth of Women's Liberation in America* (New York, Wm. Morrow, 1986); citations are from the paperback edition (New York, Warner Books, 1987) with an afterword.
3. *Ibid.,* 146.
4. *Ibid,* 148.

The Hidden History of the E.R.A.

Chapter 1. The Two Kinds of Feminism

1. J. Stanley Lemons, *The Woman Citizen, Social Feminism in the 1920s* (Urbana, Univ. of Illinois Press, 1973). This is the authoritative treatment of this ill-understood but fateful period.
2. Summary based on Samuel Yellen, *American Labor Struggles* (N.Y., Harcourt Brace, 1936, repr. S. A. Russell, 1956), Chap. 6, esp. 171f; and P. S. Foner, *History of the Labor Movement in the United States* (N.Y., International Pub., 1947+), 4:315f.

Chapter 2. The Original Alliance for the E.R.A.

1. For the B.R.T. case, see Lemons, *op. cit.* (1: n.1).
2. For instance: Foner, *Women and the American Labor Movement* (N.Y., Free Press, 1979), 2:93–95.
3. Letter, W. Seibert, Superintendent of Surface Transportation, to J. J. Dempsey, Vice-President, B.R.T. Co., June 12, 1919; in National Woman's Party, *Papers,* Reel No. 3.
4. Mary Anderson, testimony, House Judiciary Committee, February 1925, page 58.
5. Lemons, *op. cit.* (1: n.1), 143f.
6. *Ibid.,* 191.
7. *Ibid.,* 193; he is also quoting "Second Women's Industrial Conference and the Assaults Upon It," *Life and Labor Bulletin,* IV (Feb. 1926), p. 2.
8. These samples of Mrs. Belmont's thinking are from her article in the *Ladies Home Journal,* September 1922.
9. Lemons, *op. cit.* (1: n.1), 182.
10. For Alice Paul's taped memoirs, see Alice Paul, "Conversations with Alice Paul: Woman's Suffrage and the Equal Rights Amendment," Regional Oral History Office, Bancroft Library, University of California, Berkeley, 1975. Unpublished typescript; interview conducted by Amelia Fry. Quoted here by the kind permission of the Director of the Bancroft Library. Re Maud Younger, see pages 430–32.
11. Florence Kelley quoted in Josephine Goldmark, *Impatient Crusader,* 181f.

Chapter 3. Two Women

1. Unless otherwise noted, this account of Florence Kelley's life is based on her own autobiographical series of articles in *The Survey,* four issues, Oct. 1, 1926, and Feb. 1, Apr. 1, and June 1, 1927; and citations are drawn from this source too.

2.Florence Kelley, "Should Women Be Treated Identically with Men by the Law?" in *American Review,* March–April 1923; quoted in Goldmark, *op. cit.*(2: n.9), 184f.

3. National Consumers League, *Annual Report* (N.Y., 1902), p. 3; Quoted in Allis Rosenberg Wolfe, "Women, Consumerism, and the National Consumers League in the Progressive Era, 1900–1923," in *Labor History,* 16, Summer 1975, p. 380.

4.Goldmark, *op. cit.* (2: n.9), 182.

5.This and subsequent passages from Alice Paul's oral memoirs come from: "Conversations with Alice Paul...," *op. cit.* (2: n.10).

6.Besides Paul's oral memoirs, see also Lemons, *op. cit.* (1: n.1), 183f.

7.For this line of thought in Hewlett, see her book (*op. cit.* Pref.: n.2).

Chapter 4. Wisconsin Demonstrates the E.R.A.

1.Lemons, *op. cit.* (1: n.1), 187.

2.Petition and Statement of Facts for consideration of the Wisconsin Industrial Commission by men and women of the state: who are vitally interested in the welfare of women workers in the industries of Wisconsin." January 1917. Submitted by J. J. Handley, Secretary, Wisconsin Federation of Labor; H. H. Jacobs, President, Executive Committee of Milwaukee Council of Social Agencies; Sophie Gudden, Wisconsin Consumers League; available in State of Wisconsin Legislative Reference Library.

3.Chapter 529, Wisconsin Laws, 1921. See also shorter excerpt in Lemons, *op. cit.* (1: n.1), 187.

4.Mabel Raef Putnam, *The Winning of the First Bill of Rights for American Women* (Milwaukee, F. Putnam, 1924), p.

5.Esther Dunshee, "Blanket Legislation," in *Ohio Woman Voter,* May 1926, p. 3.

6.Putnam, *op. cit.* (4: n.4), 24f, also 15.

7.*Ibid.,* p. 48f; see also Lemons, *op. cit.* (1: n.1), 188.

8The last four paragraphs: "Report of Wisconsin Women's Committee on Study of Chapter 529, Wisconsin Laws 1921, Women's Equal Rights Law," September 23, 1922. Found in Wisconsin League of Women Voters subject file, Archives and Manuscripts Division of Wisconsin State Historical Society. See also Lemons, *op. cit.* (1: n.1), 188.

9.Industrial Commission of Wisconsin, *Wisconsin Labor Market,* June 1923, p. 8; January 1926, p. 17; December 1927, p. 14.

10.(1) Edwin E. Witte, *History and Purposes of the Wisconsin Women's Equal Rights Law (including court decisions construing this law),* 1928–1929 (Wisconsin Legislative Reference Library, Madison, December 1929). — (2) Howard F. Ohm, same title (same publisher, July 1938).

11.Putnam, *op. cit.* (4: n.4), 67f.

12.For another, similar formulation of Ekern's argument see the source cited by Lemons, *op. cit.* (1: n.1), 189.

13.Letter, Herman Ekern to Mabel Putnam, January 27, 1923; found in Legislative Reference Library, Madison, portfolio #328.15W75z.

14.Leaflet, "Special Privileges for Women," by the National Woman's Party, 1925; in Legislative Reference Library, *ibid.* (preceding note).

Chapter 5. The Investigation: Facts Versus Claims

1.Unless otherwise noted, the source is the Women's Bureau *Bulletin* No. 65, "The Effects of Labor Legislation on the Employment Opportunities of Women," Washington, D.C., 1928.

2.On the B.R.T. case, see Chap. 2, p. 15f.

3.See Women's Bureau *Bulletin* No. 15, "Some Effects of Legislation Limiting Hours of Work for Women," Washington, D.C., 1921.

4.Women's Bureau *Bulletin* No. 11, "Women Street Car Conductors and Ticket Agents," Washington, D.C., 1921. — Dept. of Labor. Bureau of Women in Industry. Brief submitted to the State Industrial Commission, New York, June 17, 1919.

5.This passage is from *Bulletin* No. 11, the first listed in the preceding note.

6.Lemons, op. cit. (1: n.1), 195. The beneficial effects of "protective" legislation for women were also documented in Mary Elizabeth Pidgeon, *Women in the Economy of the U.S.A.*

7.Lemons, *ibid.,* 196.

Chapter 6. The "Right to Work" Ploy

1.Michael Rogin, "Voluntarism..." in Charles M. Rehmus and Doris B. McLaughlin, eds. *Labor and American Politics,* 122.

2.This and the preceding quotation from Philip S. Foner, *History of the Labor Movement in the U.S.,* 5:129, 130.

3.See the historical sketch on "The Minimum Wage" in *The American Labor Year Book 1919–1920,* ed. by Alexander Trachtenberg (N.Y., Rand School,

1920), 240f. For "government paternalism," see Foner, *op. cit.* (6: n.2), 6:134.

4.This debate was published in the magazine *Forum,* August 1924.

5.Gail Loughlin is here quoted from the *Congressional Digest,* March 1924.

6.Blatch and Beyer are quoted from *The Nation,* January 31, 1923.

7.*Survey* (magazine), March 15, 1919.

8.Lemons, *op. cit.* (1: n.1), 199; see also pages following.

9.From a historical note "The Federation Story" in the organization's organ, the *National Business Woman,* July 1957.

10.Shulamith Firestone, *The Dialectics of Sex* (N.Y., Bantam, 1971, 1970), 37 and 20–21.

Chapter 7. The Stakes and the Players

1.This was reported in the B.P.W. organ *Independent Woman,* September 1952; the italics pointing to *unqualified* as the crucial word are added.

2.The speaker was Myra Wolfgang; the debate program was the PBS "The Advocates," in 1972.

3.Grace Hutchins, *Women Who Work* (New York, 1952).

4.Letter, Richard Nixon to Helen Lee MacKellar, March 3, 1950; letter, Mildred Palmer to Natalie Shaffer, May 29, 1950; letter, Gerald Ford to Mrs. Stapleton Pelletier, February 27, 1950 — all in the N.W.P., *Papers,* Reel no. 96.

Chapter 8. The E.R.A. Murder Case

1.Ethel E. Murrell, article in the American Bar Association *Journal,* January 1952.

2.*Colliers,* August 19, 1950.

3.The quotation from Rep. St. George is from the *Journal of the American Association of University Women,* May 1952.

4.*Congressional Record,* January 25, 1950, p. 868.

5.See *Congressional Record* for January 23 and 25, 1950.

6.Alice Paul, "Conversations with Alice Paul...," *op. cit.* (2: n.10). The next excerpt from the memoirs is on page 518.

7.Letter, Florence Armstrong to N.W.P. Officers, National Council Members, and Committee Chairmen, January 25, 1950; in N.W.P. *Papers,* Reel no. 96.

8.Letter, Emma Guffey Miller to Dr. Agnes Wells, February 22, 1950, *ibid.*

9.Letter, Marjorie Longwell to Alice Paul, February 2, 1950, *ibid.*

10. Letter, Katherine St. George to Mrs. George T. Vickers, January 31, 1950, *ibid.*

11.Letter, Anita Pollitzer to a "friend," February 26, 1950, *ibid.*

12.Letters to Alice Paul: by Olive Lacy, March 15, 1950, and by Jane Norman Smith, March 27, 1950, *ibid.*

13. Letter, Elizabeth Forbes to Agnes Wells, March 18, 1950, *ibid.*

14. Letter, Alice Paul to Anita Pollitzer, March 12, 1950, ibid.

15. In this connection, for example, see the letter, Anita Pollitzer to "Ernestine," March 9, 1950, *ibid.*

16."Conversations with Alice Paul...," *op. cit.* (2: n.10), p. 518.

17. Minutes of National Council Meeting, December 10, 1950, N.W.P., *Papers,* Reel no. 115.

18. *Congressional Record,* July 16, 1953, p. 8955.

Chapter 9. Title VII Takes the Trick

1. For this material, see *Congressional Record,* July 2, 1960, p. 15679–15686.

2. Robert W. Smuts, *Women and Work in America,* (N.Y., Schocken, 1971), xii.

3."Equal Rights Is Battle Cry," Columbus (Ohio) *Dispatch,* February 12, 1967, in N.W.P. *Papers,* Reel no. 172.

4.Raymond J. Celada, "Equal Employment Opportunity: A Legislative History and Analysis of Title VII of the Civil Rights Act of 1984," presented at hearings before the House General Subcommittee on Labor of the Committee on Education and Labor, July 21, 1965, p116–131 (Washington, D.C., 1965).

5."Equal Rights Is Battle Cry," *loc. cit.* (9: n.3).

6.See the reference to Wolfgang above, Chap. 7, p. 52.

Chapter 10. How the Pure E.R.A. Won — and Lost

1.A useful survey of state-by-state labor legislation for women as of 1969, that is, at that time not yet destroyed through Title VII, may be found in the *Congressional Record* for August 10, 1970, pages 28007–11.

Chapter 11. On the Fourteenth Route

1.Letter, Ethel Adamson to Alice Paul, December 22, 1938, in N.W.P. *Papers,* Reel no. 62.

2.Letter, Caroline Lexow Babcock to Ethel Adamson, January 1, 1939, *ibid.,* Reel no. 63.

3.For Bayh, see the *Congressional Record,* January 28, 1971.

4.The quotation from Ervin is from his statement before the House Judiciary Committee of March 23, 1971.

5.The paper by Prof. Kanowitz was published in the *Congressional Record,* September 14, 1970, and reprinted in the *New Mexico Law Review,* July 1971, from which it is quoted here.

6.The information about Griffiths given in the last sentence comes from Paul Mode, who was then Bayh's legislative assistant for the E.R.A., given orally to one of the authors (Diamond).

7.This account is in part based on conversations between one of the authors (Diamond) and Catherine East, Marguerite Rawalt, and Paul Mode. Also see Isabelle Shelton, "How Equal Rights Passed Senate," *Washington Sunday Star,* March 26, 1972.

8.Re Paul Mode, see above, n.3.

9.Letter, Gladys O'Donnell to Senator Bayh, October 26, 1970, in N.W.P. *Papers,* Reel no. 112.

10.This is cited from the letter to Senator Cook, same date, *loc. cit.*

11.News Release, National Federation of Republican Women, November 10, 1970; in N.W.P. *Papers,* Reel no. 112. — The *New York Times* story of November 12 referred to a meeting held on November 11 to issue the press release.

12.Bulletin, National Ad Hoc Committee ERA; in N.W.P. *Papers,* Reel no. 112.

13.N.O.W. statement of November 13, 1970; *loc. cit.*

14.The hostile observer is Marguerite Rawalt, a past president of B.P.W.; see above, n.7.

15.Letter, Phyllis Wetherby to Senator Bayh, November 17, 1970; *loc. cit.* (above n.12).

16.Senator Bayh in *Congressional Record,* November 16, 1970, p. 37268.

Chapter 12. How They Snatched Defeat from the Jaws of Victory

1.Hewlett, *op. cit.* (Pref., n.2), 198.

2.*Ibid.,* 202f.

3.Senator John Tower, speech before the American Bar Association, August 10, 1970; text released from his Senate office; in N.W.P. *Papers,* Reel no. 112.

4.Letter, Senator John Tower to S. Diamond, July 14, 1981.

Appendix: The California Experience

1.This article, written December 1971, was published in various California trade-union papers with slight variations; and also in the "Forum" section of the Bay

Area *Guardian,* April 12, 1972, to criticize that paper's endorsement of the Pure E.R.A. position.

2.The quotation is from Aileen Hernandez's "Open Letter to the California Federation of Labor..." dated May 20, 1972, signed by Hernandez as Chairone of the National Advisory Committe of N.O.W.

3.M. I. Miller and H. Linker, "State Politics and Public Interests," in *Society,* May–June 1974. Our summaries here, as indicated, involve some condensation. Miller-Linker add that there was another argument used, based on the technicalities of the 1971 Sail' er Inn decision of the California Supreme Court, but that the E.R.A. proponents did not "rely heavily" on it; so perhaps we can be spared its legal complications.

4.Mary Mabry's letter appeared in the union's organ, *The Rebel,* February 24, 1971, reprinted from the Vancouver (Washington) *Columbian.*

5.Diane Watson, president of the local N.O.W. organization, debated Anne Draper in Berkeley on April 1, 1972. Copies of the tape were available from Union W.A.G.E. for a while afterward; the passage given here is cited from this tape.

6.The bulletin of N.O.W.'s Sacramento office was *Capitol Alert,* March 31, 1972.

Index

215

--

Made in the USA
San Bernardino, CA
07 July 2014